MW01234848

Up from Slavery

Up from Slavery

A History from

Slavery to City Hall

In New England

THIRMAN L. MILNER

Pleasant Word
PW A Division of WinePress Group

Pleasant Word (a division of WinePress Publishing, PO Box 428, Enumclaw, WA 98022) functions only as book publisher. As such, the ultimate design, content, editorial accuracy, and views expressed or implied in this work are those of the author.

Unless otherwise noted, all Scriptures are taken from the *Holy Bible, New International Version®, NIV®*. Copyright © 1973, 1978, 1984 by Biblica, Inc.™ Used by permission of Zondervan. All rights reserved worldwide.

Scripture references marked KJV are taken from the *King James Version* of the Bible.

Scripture references marked NASB are taken from the *New American Standard Bible*, © 1960, 1963, 1968, 1971, 1972, 1973, 1975, 1977 by The Lockman Foundation. Used by permission.

ISBN 13: 978-1-4141-1527-6
ISBN 10: 1-4141-1527-X
Library of Congress Catalog Card Number: 2009906682

Contents

Acknowledgments

WHY NOT WAS the slogan that I used for my first campaign for mayor of the city of Hartford, Connecticut. Why Not Milner For Mayor became a successful campaign and rallying call. To those of you with aggressive ambitions, determined desires, or grandiose goals, never say can't but Why Not?

I dedicate this book to generations that preceded me, from the early days of slavery up to the present. Enduring untold hardships through sweat and labor, these men and women paved the way for me and many others. They left footprints in the sands of life for us to follow and stood tall with courage against all odds, saying, "Why Not?" when others asked why?

This book is also dedicated to my mother and father, Grace Stewart Milner Allen and Henry Marshall Milner. When I was only three years old, my mother became a single parent due to my father being hospitalized; he remained in hospital and died there when I was twelve. My mother died in 1984 at the age of 83. My father, whom I knew little about because of his hospitalization, fought in the first World War. After marrying my mother, they had nine children. He was one of the few African Americans in Hartford at that time to have his own business.

I also acknowledge some of those who played a role in my life.

- My grandmothers, Elizabeth Milner and Florence Stewart

- My brothers and sister. My oldest brother, Marshall, and the third oldest, Albert, are both deceased, as well as my sister, Shirley, the youngest of the family who died a year before my mother; my brother Stanton, who was the family historian and saved family information and most of my political records; Nelson and Gary, who still live in the Hartford area.

- My children and stepchildren. Theresa, who was as close as any daughter could be, and her brother, my son, Gary Rogers; stepchildren Ray, Manuel, Joseph and Virginia Monteiro.

- My nephew and godson, Anthony Milner, who at the time of this writing is an assistant chief of the Hartford Fire Department. He was partly raised by his mother, my mother, and me and who became my special nephew.

- My grandchildren, Anthony, Wayne, Shawneka, Shawnea, Reene, Antwan, and Dominique Rogers, my great grandchildren,

- My godchild and niece who I am very proud of, Danielle Milner, daughter of another of my special nephews, Hartford firefighter, Duane Milner, a good friend and confidant, who keeps an eye on me.

- My Aunt Flossie and her son, Chester, who became a popular funeral director in New York, both now deceased. His sister, Pat Harris, who devoted her life to help him until he passed and then moved on to her own career.

- My niece, Dalia May, who has contributed greatly to this book.

- My niece, Signe Milner-Martin, daughter of my oldest brother, Marshall, who was my proofreader.

- My niece, Nina Milner, oldest daughter of my brother, Albert, a nurse who became somewhat of a daughter to me after her father's death. Thank you for being there for me during periods of my illnesses as well as a dear companion, along with her mother, Dorothy, who sometimes came along with us on fun trips.

- To the group we called *The Mayor's Crew*: Anthony Napoleon, my former executive assistant in the mayor's office, and my executor and close friend; Ruth Hall, now deceased, who I called "the love of my life," because of our close and sincere relationship; Barbara Wiggins, my newly found cousin and close friend; Roberta Jones, my niece by marriage; Debra Callis, a retired Hartford police detective and special friend; and Tina McDonald, with whom I share my birth date. These close friends were my eyes and ears during my term as mayor and have remained a "crew" ever since.

- To my early supporters who were with me throughout my political career, and beyond.

- Jim Monroe, now deceased, entrepreneur and my first political advisor, supporter, friend, and even boss, as I once worked for his local home oil delivery service as office manager.

- To Curtis Robinson, a successful businessman, whom I have known for many years, an early supporter, and friend who is also a financial backer of this book. Curtis is a successful entrepreneur, and during my term as mayor he graciously allowed me to host a weekly radio talk show *The Mayor's Corner* in his restaurant *The Staircase Lounge* in downtown Hartford, where guests would call in or come in and have brunch with me for an hour. After leaving the mayor's office, I took a part-time position handling the insurance needs of several of his successful companies.

- John Allen, editor and chief of Hartford's oldest Black newspaper *The Northend Agents,* a weekly community newspaper in which I wrote a column for more than 26 years. John was an early supporter dating back to when I first ran for state representative.

- Joy Rodman, Edgar Richards, John Fulse, Jeffrey Pounds, Craig Stallings, Gregory Perkins, and Anthony McCann, all who served as staff during my terms in public office, as well as my high school coach, good friend, and advisor to this day, Bill Faber of Glastonbury, Connecticut.

- I must acknowledge another friend and financial backer of this book, Greenwich, Connecticut businessman Ned Lamont, who I supported for governor of our state and who was a supporter of mine in my last bid for the mayor's office. Ned is a friend and an individual dedicated to the concerns of the people and the concerns of our state and nation.

- To all those I've mentioned and many more who were/are my supporters, advisors, staff, confidants, relatives, and friends. There are far too many of you to mention, but you're such an important part of my life. This book is dedicated to all of you with gratitude and thanksgiving.

CHAPTER 1

The Research Begins

WHERE TO BEGIN? I can trace my family's history back to the slavery era in the United States. Court documents trace my family roots, on my mother's side, to Middlesex County, Connecticut. My sincere thanks goes to Judith Ellen Johnson who, in the late 1900's, as a staff genealogist with the Connecticut Historical Society, in Hartford, Connecticut, personally contributed her time and effort to trace my family's history. Using just a suitcase left by my grandmother, a list of names, one family letter, two family albums handed down from my grandmother, and from what little family oral history that I had written about in a Hartford African American community newspaper called the *Northend Agents*, Judith painstakingly reconstructed my family tree. She then wrote the following:

Normally, when you trace a family history, you begin with the present generation and work backward. However, for my purpose I'd like to begin with a lady named Abigail Stanton Stewart, Mayor Milner's maternal great-grandmother. Abigail Stanton Stewart has been the keystone in my research. Besides being a remarkable woman in her own way, she was also a saver, and the materials the family has shared have provided me not only with a sense of Abigail's personality, but the answers to some of my research problems as well.

Abigail Stanton came to Hartford as early as 1860, where, according to the 1860 census, she and her mother, Abigail, were listed in the household of the recently married William B. Smith and his wife, Virginia, a Hartford couple with whose family the Stantons would have a long association. They may have found this position through young Abigail's brother, Chester C. Stanton, who, according to the Hartford City Directory, was working for Mr. Smith in 1869. It is not clear where she met her husband, or how long she stayed in Hartford, but in 1869, in Middletown, Abigail Stanton married Albert E. Stewart, a native of New Orleans, Louisiana, who had probably migrated to Connecticut after the Civil War. According to the Middletown City directories, the Stewarts lived in that city until 1878. During those years Albert Stewart worked in a variety of positions including a coachman, hackman, and laborer. While never listed in the city directories, several family records also revealed that Albert had a business selling ice cream.

Sometime during 1878 Albert and Abigail Stewart moved to Hartford and took up residence at 116 Albany Avenue. The 1886 and 1887 directories contained listings not only for Albert but also for Abigail, who apparently had begun her own business as a laundress. The next few years must have brought changes to the Stewart household; by 1891 it seems that Albert and Abby were living apart from one another.

In 1892 Abby moved from 116 Albany to 10 Green Street with her son Henry B. Stewart, the only one of Abby's five children to survive beyond the age of twenty, and by 1893 Albert Stewart was no longer listed in the Hartford directory. Abby and her son remained at the Green Street address until 1900, during which time Henry B. Stewart married Florence L. Thompson of Hartford and started raising a family that would ultimately, like his mother's, number five children, three boys born by 1900, and two girls shortly after.

Sometimes in researching a family's history you find that the events of one generation parallel another. Albert and Abigail Stewart's fourth child was a little girl who, unfortunately, died a month after she was born. Abby named this daughter Grace. The fourth child of Henry and Florence Stewart was also a little girl named Grace, who was more fortunate than her namesake, and grew up to become the mother of Hartford's first Black mayor.

Between 1900 and 1910, Abigail Stewart was not listed in the Hartford city directories. Although the old Hartford directories had a section that reported peoples' migrations out of the city, Abby's move was not reported. At that time many of the smaller communities did not have directories, but fortunately for me Abby Stewart saved many cards and letters from family and friends. For instance a letter postmarked the 28th of September, 1907, was addressed to Abby Stewart in care of her daughter-in-law in Windsor, Connecticut. In this letter Charlie Beaman of Middletown, an old family friend, expressed his condolences to Abby on the loss of her brother, Chester.

If I may digress from Abby's story, I'd like to talk about Chester for a few minutes. Charlie Beaman's sympathy letter triggered some research on Chester Stanton, leading me to some very interesting information. At the time of Chester's death, rarely did members of the minority communities, black or white, warrant more than a brief death notice in the local papers. Chester Stanton, however, was an exception. When he died on September 22nd, 1907, his death was noted in an extensive obituary in the *Hartford Courant*.

Chester had a long association with the Governor's Foot Guard, but even though he was listed in the Hartford City Directory from 1858 to 1868, and again from 1877 through 1907, nothing in his occupational listings gave any indication of his 25 or so years with the Foot Guard. However, his affiliation with this group was clear through his obituary, and through the funeral memorabilia that Abby Stewart had saved.

Throughout his entries in the city directories, Chester was listed as a laborer, porter, gardener, and driver. While in the employment of

William B. Smith, he was an "ostler" an old term for someone who took care of horses. Perhaps as early as 1888, but definitely by 1899, Chester had his own cab business.

Why Abby Stewart moved to Windsor and what she did while she was there is unclear. By 1910 she was back in Hartford living at 94 Ann Street, the residence of Rebecca Morgan Brainard, in whose employment Abby remained until Miss Brainard's death in 1917 at the age of 90. It was during these years—in 1914 to be precise—that Abby suffered her final loss as a mother. On the 20th of May, 1914, Henry B. Stewart, Abby's only surviving child, died in New Haven, Connecticut, of tuberculosis.

From 1918 to 1919, Abby's mail was sent to her in East Windsor in the care of Miss Sarah Coleman. By 1920 Abby had returned to Hartford, this time residing at 106 Brown Street with the family of Morris Mitchell, a porter for the Sisson drug company. For the first time Abby was listed in the city directory as the widow of Albert Stewart.

Up to this point what had happened to Albert Stewart had been a complete mystery; when he disappeared from the Hartford directories, there was no indication of what happened to him. The directories listed Abby as "Mrs. Abigail Stewart, laundress," not "Mrs. Abigail Stewart, widow," nor was she listed as a widow in the 1900 or 1910 census. Up to that point I hadn't been able to find Albert Stewart on the 1900 census, nor had I located a death certificate for him in Hartford or Middletown. Abby's 1920 directory listing was the first mention of Albert in a 28-year period. The mystery finally unraveled when the Milner family brought in an old suitcase full of Abby's belongings. Among some papers in the suitcase was a bill dated Nov. 26, 1919, from the J. C. Lincoln Company of Willimantic for the burial expenses of Albert Stewart, who had died at St. Joseph Hospital in Windham on November 10th. A quick check of the Willimantic city directories revealed that, when Albert left Hartford an 1893, he moved to Willimantic where he remained for the rest of his life.

Besides being the year that Abby was first listed as a widow, 1920 was also a census year. Abby's entry in the 1920 census listed her in a household headed by Henry and Margaret Green, including Morris Mitchell and his wife, and among others, Abby's granddaughter, Grace. Abby and Grace remained with the Mitchells at 106 Brown Street until 1924, when on January 20th, two days shy of her 23rd birthday, Grace Nelson Stewart married Marshall Milner and established her own household. For the next thirteen years, Abby made her home with Grace and Marshall Milner, until on the 22nd of May, 1937, when Abigail Stanton Stewart, at the age of 89, passed from this life.

Abigail Stanton Stewart spent the better part of 60 years of her life in Hartford but she was not born there, nor was her birth ever recorded. She is the person who brought this family to Hartford; she is also the bridge to their past.

Based on her marriage record and the ages given in several other records, Abby was born in Middletown between 1845 and 1848, and probably on May 15th. On Abby's death certificate, Grace Milner listed Abby's parents as Samuel V. Stanton and Abigail, with the name Peters and a question mark, Mrs. Milner wasn't sure. The 1850 census for Middletown listed a Samuel V. Stanton with a wife whose first name was Abigail. Included amongst the six children in the household were a son, Chester, aged thirteen, and a daughter Abigail, aged five.

The census further indicated that the Stanton family owned property. It was on Cross Street in Middletown, and is incorrectly listed as the C. Stanton Estate on the 1874 map of Middletown. There is an 1871 deed to this property, which can best be described as a genealogist's dream because of the information it provides linking Abby to her parents, and a couple of other people as well. The grantors of this deed are Abigail Stanton of Middletown and Chester C. Stanton of Hartford; the grantee, if Abigail Stewart, is identified as the "daughter of said Abigail Stanton, sister of said Chester and wife of Albert Stewart." The property description in this deed refers to "other land of the estate of Samuel V. Stanton" and ends with the statement "our interest in the aforesaid premises being derived as heirs at law of the said Samuel V. Stanton."

Abby's father, Samuel V. Stanton, left only a few records to tell us who he was or what he did in his life. Like his daughter, Abigail, Samuel's birth was not recorded. However, his marriage was, and in this record I also learned his wife's maiden name. On February 14, 1835, Samuel V. Stanton of Middletown married Abigail Caples, also of Middletown. In 1835 Middletown included not only Middletown as it is today, but also the present towns of Portland, East Hampton, Cromwell, and Middlefield. Samuel and Abigail were married by James Noyes, Pastor of the Third Congregational Church in Middletown, which was probably Abigail Caples' church. The Third Congregational Church of Middletown was actually in Middlefield. Samuel and Abigail may also have been married in a double ceremony, for if you look at the next entry on the page you will see recorded, on the same date and by the same minister, the marriage of Ezekiel Caples, Abigail's brother, and Harriet Beaman.

For at least part of his life, Samuel Stanton worked as a day laborer, judging from the account books of William Lyman, a Middlefield farmer and active abolitionist, which are in the collections of the Middlesex County Historical Society in Middletown. Connecticut's economy through the middle of the 19th century was based on the barter system, trading goods for services or vice versa. William Lyman probably purchased these supplies for Samuel Stanton in return for which Samuel agreed to work for Lyman at rates ranging from $12 to $15 per month. There are several entries of this sort for Samuel from 1835 until 1839, when Samuel settled his account with William Lyman and probably moved into Middletown proper.

On Dec. 4, 1851, Samuel's then youngest son, John, died at the age of 11. The local undertaker at the time was J. B. Southmayd, and the expenses to Samuel for the funeral of his son can be found in the Southmayd account books, which have been deposited at the Godfrey Library in Middletown.

Samuel himself died in 1856 at, according to his death record, 44 years of age. His death certificate is typical of the time period, giving virtually no personal information, but by using his age of 39 on the 1850 census and his age at death of 44, we can figure a birth year somewhere between 1810 and 1812. The Southmayd funeral records might have provided a little more information; unfortunately, the account books for the years 1853 through 1880 are missing. However, according to the first volume of burial records in the Middletown Health Department, Samuel Stanton was buried by J.B. Southmayd, probably in the Washington Street Cemetery.

Since he had no birth record, and his death record provided no information, finding parents for Samuel V. Stanton required some detective work. On the 1840 census for Middletown, Samuel Stanton was listed next to a woman named Rachel Stanton, who according to the statistics and columns, was somewhere between 36 and 55 years of age. On the 1850 census, Rachel Stanton and Samuel Stanton were separated by one family, but still living very close to one another. In 1850, Rachel Stanton was listed as 58 years old and Samuel, 39. Women are known to have shaved several years off their ages in the census, so Rachel could easily have been more than 58 years old. However, even if she were 58, that made her 19 years older than Samuel, and old enough to be his mother. Rachel Stanton had virtually no vital statistics recorded in Middletown, not even a death certificate, but in 1850 Rachel's household included a young man named George Stanton.

In the Southmayd account book for 1851 – 1853, an entry was made on October 29, 1851, billing Rachel Stanton for the funeral expenses of her son, George G. Stanton, aged 31. There are a couple of things to note about this entry. Between Rachel's name and the debtor column the word "estate" is squeezed in, in a lighter ink, indicating that it was added to the entry later. Below the entry for George is another one, dated April 18th, for a funeral whose expenses included a coffin with a plate indicating that its occupant was 69 years old.

Since the April entry followed the October one, I checked the local newspaper for April of 1852 and found that the second funeral was that of Rachel Stanton who died on April 17, 1852. Rachel's expenses were apparently not billed to another individual, and the word "estate" that had been slipped in told me to check for a probate record. In the Middletown Probate Court, I found that Rachel had written a will and had named as her son, Samuel V. Stanton.

At this point, Rachel's husband and Samuel's father is still a mystery. So far I have found no marriage record for Rachel, and there is no indication that she was anyone's widow in her probate records, so I can only present a possibility. To date the best candidate is John or Jack Stanton, assuming they are one and the same person. The evidence is weak and inconclusive. There was a John Stanton listed in the 1820 census for Middletown, who was clearly a black man; located at the Connecticut Sate Library, are the account books of Ebenezer Tracy, a Middletown physician, in which there are entries dated March 28th, and April 5th, 1821, for Jack Stanton. The Middlesex County Historical Society has a collection of bills to the city of Middletown which include one from Caleb Griffin, dated April 22, 1822, for digging Jack Stanton's grave, and another submitted in 1823 by Eleazer Barnes for a coffin made for Jack Stanton on April 3, 1822. Unfortunately, there is nothing in these records that indicates any kind of relationship between Jack Stanton and Rachel.

As for Rachel Stanton herself, the few records that exist for her are quite interesting. The fact that Rachel left a will disposing of her modest estate is unusual for a mid-19th century black woman, and her estate included a house and land, which she left to her surviving children and grandchildren. There are no deeds recording the transfer of Rachel's property to her children because it was passed through probate. But there was a deed recorded when Rachel received the property, and this deed is another genealogist's dream. On July 2, 1828, Martha Mortimer Starr entered this deed into the Middletown Land Records, from which I have abstracted the following.

Know all men by these presents that I, Martha Mortimer Starr, otherwise known as Martha Mortimer of Middletown in the State of Connecticut, because I know it was the desire of my Father and Mother as well as that of the late Philip Mortimer Esq., that the land hereinafter mentioned should belong to Jack Mortimer and after his death to his children, do, by these presents, give, release, and forever quit claim unto Amaryllis Bean and Rachel Stanton, children of Jack Mortimer and to Mary Conny and John Conny, children of Silva Mortimer who was a child of said Jack Mortimer and to their heirs and assigns, all such right, title and interest as the said Martha has in a certain piece of land with the buildings there on, formerly occupied by the said Jack Mortimer.

To have and to hold in the following portions: to Amaryllis Bean, Rachel Stanton and Charles Mortimer (who, the clerk notes was not listed earlier in the deed) one undivided fourth part to each and to Mary Conny and John Conny as representing their mother one fourth part.

CHAPTER 2

From Slavery, the Mortimers

JUDITH CONTINUES.

Martha Mortimer Starr has an interesting story herself, which probably accounts for the timing of this deed. By fulfilling her parent's wishes, she left us a record of at least some of Rachel's family, and a clue to their origins.

Martha Mortimer Starr was the adopted granddaughter of Philip Mortimer, Esq., described in the Starr genealogy as a "gentleman of wealth." Philip was married, but he and his wife, Martha, had no children of their own, so Philip adopted his niece, Ann.

Catherine Carnall, the wife of George Starr, was the mother of Martha Mortimer Starr.

In the 1790 census, Philip Mortimer was listed as living alone with a household of eleven slaves. Philip Mortimer was a devout member of the Episcopal Church, and in the records of what is now Holy Trinity Church in Middletown, we find that Philip tended to what he considered the spiritual needs of his servants by having them baptized in his faith. The records of Philip's servants are found as early as 1752 and as late as 1793. Unfortunately, nowhere in these records is there any mention of the servants' parents, or what, if any, family relationships existed among them. For example, on November 21, 1773, Rachel and Silva, servant children of Philip Mortimer, were baptized. There is no indication of a relationship or names of their parents. There are several child or infant servants named Rachel baptized in Philip Mortimer's household, and I think the Rachel baptized on May 26, 1793, is probably Rachel Stanton. On April 28, 1771, two adult servants named Will and John were baptized, and it's very possible that this John later became known as "Jack."

Philip Mortimer died in 1794, leaving a large estate, including a will and two inventories. In his will Philip Mortimer provided very clear instructions for the manumission of his servants, including a woman named Sophie and her husband, Jack, a woman named Amaryllis, and a woman named Silva. Rachel and Charles were not mentioned for a very simple reason: the will was written on July 9, 1792, and neither of them had yet been born. The inventory of Philip Mortimer's estate was exhibited on October 27, 1794, and there, amongst the list of servants, we find Rachel listed as a girl child. The Starr family contested Philip Mortimer's will, delaying the settlement of the estate for several years, and by the time the second inventory was filed in 1796, it was clearly evident that some of the servants had either died or been freed.

What happened to Jack after the death of Philip Mortimer is largely a guess because of lack of documentation. We know he adopted his master's surname, and I suspect he continued to work for the Starr family. The death of his wife, Sophie, in 1807, was entered in the record of the First Congregational Church in Middletown. Jack may be the John Mortimer listed here in the 1810 census for Middletown, and he and Rachel were mentioned in the accounts of Dr. Ebenezer Tracy. Though not listed in the census, he was alive in 1820 as is evident in the inventory of the joint estate of George and Ann Starr, dated September, 1820. This inventory included "the house and lot now occupied by Jack Mortimer," but he was clearly dead by July 2, 1828, when Martha Mortimer Starr gave the property intended for Jack Mortimer to his heirs.

For the final chapter in this story, we must turn to Abigail Caples, the wife of Samuel V. Stanton, and the mother of Abigail Stanton Stewart. Another photo of this lady in the Milner albums is identified as "Abigail Stanton." Since this is too old a photograph to be Abby Stewart, it's probably safe to assume that this lady is Abigail Caples Stanton.

Abigail Stanton had a marriage certificate, which identified her as a Caples and a death certificate containing no parental information. She had no birth or baptismal record. She was listed in the 1850 census in Middletown, the 1860 census in Hartford, and the 1870 census again in Middletown. She was the grantor on three deeds in the Middletown Land Records, one to the African Methodist Episcopal Church, and two to her daughter, Abigail Stewart. She was also listed in the Middletown city directories from 1868 through 1873. In 1860, the probate court appointed her guardian of Samuel's niece, Fannie M. Stanton, and in 1871 she was appointed guardian of her own son, John Samuel Stanton. She was the mother of at least eight children, all but two of whom predeceased her. Abigail Caples Stanton died on the 27th of February 1874, at the age of 63 years, 10 months, and 27 days, giving her an approximate birth date of May 1, 1810.

So who was Abigail Caples? For once, I found a published source. In *Black Roots in Southeastern Connecticut, 1850-1900*, by Barbara W. Brown and James M. Rose, there is a section on the Caples family, and an Abigail is listed among the children of Jesse Caples and his second wife, Tamar Carter.

CHAPTER 3

Jesse Caples, the Saga Continues

JUDITH CONTINUES.

Jesse Caples has turned out to be a very interesting person. The entry in *Black Roots* indicates that Jesse was married at least three times, and he fathered at least nine children, although, given the question marks, the authors could only list three with any certainty. They also state that Jesse Caples served in the Revolution, received a pension for his service, and died in Middletown in 1847 at the age of 104 years, 6 months, and 8 days.

There is not a great deal of documentation for Jesse Caples' life, but there is some. Two of his marriages were recorded. One was in the East Hampton Church records when, in 1797 he married Tamar Carter; the other in the Middletown Vital Records, when in 1824, he married Julia Boston, here mis-transcribed as Junia Barton.

The Connecticut Historical Society has in its collections a series of diaries written by Elisha Niles, a school teacher and farmer who lived in Colchester, East Hampton, and Middle Haddam. Toward the end of his life, Niles decided to compile a list of all the students he had ever taught, and whether they were living or dead. He named amongst his pupils Jess, Robert, and Ruhamah Caples, who were probably this Jesse's children.

In Thomas Atkins' *History of Middlefield and Long Hill*, there are entries for the deaths of Jesse's wife, Tamar, as well as three of his children. And like Samuel Stanton, there are entries for Jesse Caples in the account books of William Lyman. There are also accounts for two of Jesse's sons: Chester, for whom I'm sure Chester C. Stanton was named, and Ezekiel, whose wedding to Harriet Beaman occurred the same day as Abigail Caples' wedding to Samuel V. Stanton.

The Southmayd burial records provided a conclusive link between Abigail and Jesse Caples when Samuel Stanton was billed for the funeral of his "father, Jesse Caples." Old records often left out the "in-law" designation in family relationships, and since Samuel Stanton married Abigail Caples, it was pretty safe to conclude from this record that Jesse was Abigail's father.

Jesse's death notice appeared in the *Middletown Constitution* of January 5, 1848, designating not only Jesse's advanced age but also that he was a Revolutionary War pensioner. In 1841 the government published a list of all persons listed on the 1840 census who received a pension for Revolutionary War service, and Jesse was listed as a pensioner, aged 92, living in Middletown in his own house.

Finding Jesse's pension records meant a trip to the National Archives Branch in Pittsfield, Mass., but the contents of the records made the trip more than worthwhile. Jesse's application contained a wealth of valuable information. First of all Jesse had to provide a list of his dependents and named his wife, Tamar, aged 43, his daughter, Sefrona, aged fourteen, his daughter, Abigail, aged nine, his son, Ezekiel, aged seven, his son, Frederick, aged five, his son, Chester, aged three, and an infant, seven months old.

Second he had to prove need, so he supplied an inventory of his possessions, which amounted to $58.49 and the amount of debt that he owed amounted to $55.00. He further indicated that he was "by occupation a day laborer" and "aged and rheumatic;" he was only able to work in the summer months.

Third he had to prove his service. In his application he recounted the events of his service on board a naval vessel, and then stated that he had no other evidence of his service except two documents marked A and B attached to his application. The cover on these documents indicates that they were the testimony of "two witnesses certified to be credible witnesses," a bit of an understatement, to say the least. The two men who came forward on Jesse's behalf were Dr. Phineas Hyde of Norwich, who had been the surgeon's mate on the ship, and Nathaniel Richards of New London, who had been the ship's purser.

All of this is very helpful for a researcher, not only because it gives us solid proof of Jesse Caples' family, but also because it gives Jesse some dimension as a person. However, this is only part of the story; the rest gives Jesse an incredible role in American history.

The vessel on which Jesse served was a continental frigate called the *Confederacy*. The *Confederacy*, built in Norwich, Connecticut, was a 36-gun frigate, unusual in its design and construction, and described by one source as a "beautiful but unlucky ship." Jesse Caples filed his pension application 40 years after his actual service, and, although his chronology is a little off; the details are very accurate when compared to other records of the ship's service. Abstracting from the application, Jesse stated that he "entered on board the United States Frigate *Confederacy*, at New London in the winter of the year 1779 and continued on board as a mariner and as a waiter till sometime in the month of July 1781 during which period the said ship *Confederacy* adventured on many cruises, took some valuable prizes, met with many accidents, sailed in company with the United States ships *Dean & Saratoga* and sundry other armed vessels. That the said Frigate *Confederacy* received on board Mr. Jay and family, that on her passage she lost her masts, bow sprint, and rudder on the banks of Newfoundland, bore away for Martinique where Mr. Jay and suite together with the French minister Mr. Gerard went on board a French Frigate."

Jesse's story bears up under the test of history. In his two volumes titled *History of Maritime Connecticut During the American Revolution*, Louis Middlebrook quotes the following notice published in the *Martinico Gazette* on December 16, 1779.

> The Continental Frigate *Confederacy*, 40 guns, Capt. Harding, came into our road. She left Philadelphia, October 27, 1779, destined for France, met with a gale on the banks of Newfoundland, lost her masts, had six feet of water in the hold, and arrived in the midst of perils. The Count de Gerard, late Minister from the Court of France to the United States, and his Excellency John Jay, who goes to represent the States to the Court of Madrid, were on board. They sailed from Martinico for France, Nov. 28, 1779, in the French frigate *L'Aurore*.

> The *Confederacy* remained in Martinique for nearly two months undergoing repairs. When she finally sailed back to Philadelphia, she was found to be in need of extensive refitting. After nearly eight months, she again set sail to Cape Francois in Haiti to pick up stores for the Continental Army, and began her return voyage on March 15, 1781. On April 14, 1781, the Confederacy was captured by two British vessels and escorted into New York. After refitting, we sailed for the United States, arrived at Philadelphia, underwent repairs and recruited and sailed again for Cape Francois, where we arrived with a very valuable prize. We received on board a large quantity of clothing and other necessaries for the American and French troops. On our passage home we were captured by a British Squadron in April, 1781. I was than carried to New York and put on board the Jersey prison ship where I remained until I was regularly exchanged in the month of July following, the whole time of my service embracing a period of more than two years.

For anyone who doesn't know, the Jersey prison ship was a hell hole whose captives numbered in, and perished by, the thousands. Jesse Caples spent three months on this prison ship, no doubt suffering from starvation, exposed to disease, and surrounded by death, yet he survived.

Thirman Milner's family history is far from complete. It is most definitely a genealogy in progress. There are ancestral lines into Georgia, Louisiana, and New York which haven't been traced at all. Like the Stanton's, Florence Thompson Stewart, Mayor Milner's grandmother, also has New England ancestry, but I've hit a stumbling block in Glastonbury in her grandparents' generation. There are still many questions in the Stanton and Caples families which, I hope, someday to answer. There are also all those people in the photo albums waiting to be identified.

Researching Mayor Milner's ancestors has been a delightful adventure for me, and I hope you have enjoyed hearing their stories as much as I've enjoyed bringing them to you.

CHAPTER 4

The Native American Linkage

THIRMAN MILNER TAKES over.

Judith Johnson also supplied me with a family "Pedigree Chart" that traced my family back to its Native American roots. Back in the late 1700's there was a Wongunk, Native American squaw by the name of Hannah One Penny who had a son by the name of Scipio Two Shoes. He had a son named Solomon Scipio and who was one of the parents of Jesse Caples. This part of my family history was passed down by word of mouth. Back in 2007 I wrote a short essay, a fable of sorts, as to how we gained our Native American heritage. The story was fictional and based on Hannah One Penny as a runaway slave who eventually gave birth to Scipio Two Shoes. My fictional version of this goes as follows:

Little Hannah hung close to her Mother's bosom as she was squeezed between bodies of tribal people from throughout Africa in the dark, gloomy, smelly bowels of a slave ship. She arrived in the southern part of a place now called America, only to find her Mother lying dead next to her. Fourteen-year-old Hannah found herself cold, hungry, alone, and afraid. After being dragged from the ship, she was shackled and thrown on the back of a cart and ended up on an auction block in the middle of a town square where she heard strange words, as strange looking folk with white skins gathered around listening to a man yell out as he held each slave up for sale. Little Hannah was sold to a plantation owner in a strange place in the southern part of this new land.

Early one morning, during an uprising of slaves, she escaped with several others through what was later to be called the "Underground Railroad." After long days and nights through woods, fields, dirt roads, and muddy swamps, and sometimes catching rides by hiding under dirty blankets and hay in a horse drawn cart, she ended up in a place that was much colder but where she was told that she would find freedom. Unbeknownst to her, she was in what is called a "Safe House" in a place called Connecticut. Early one evening, as she left her Safe House (a house where runaway slaves could hide in safety) to catch a breath of fresh air in this place they called "up north," she was grabbed by two strange, white skinned men. The men threw a cloth over her head, then savagely beat and raped her. Once again she found herself enslaved.

Sleeping and eating in a barn with others who were called "house" slaves, she was assigned to kitchen work. Late one night she escaped once again when she was allowed out to empty the large bucket of garbage. Barefooted on a cold winter night, with wet, white stuff falling all over her and under her feet, she ran and stumbled through the woods, hoping to find a safe haven again, a Safe House.

Not knowing where to go but knowing she had to keep going, Hannah was suddenly grabbed from behind with hands held over her mouth. Frightened, wet and freezing, she was carried to a strange place with some kind of animal tents, wood fires, and strange looking people of a different brownish color and strange looking clothing made from animal skins. She was carried into one of these tents then released. After Hannah sat down she was given food, a hot beverage, wrapped in blankets, and made welcome by several strange looking ladies dressed in these animal skins. Little did she know that she had ended up in a Native Indian tribal village.

It was a young warrior, Little Two Shoes, with his brother, who had rescued her and brought her to their family's tent, just as other Native Americans had rescued runaway slaves in the past. Little Two Shoes soon became awestruck by Hannah's smooth, darker skin, big brown eyes, and full lips. Mustering up enough courage, he soon went to his elders and asked them for her hand in marriage. Hannah, too, had found herself fascinated by this handsome, young warrior who had rescued her.

On their wedding day Hannah looked like a dark-skinned goddess to Little Two Shoes, dressed in his tribe's native wedding attire, with her hair in one long braid, topped by a white eagle feather. It was a joyous day as they went through the tribal wedding ritual and then "jumped the broom" in her native custom and feasted on wild turkey, deer, and loads of fruit and vegetables. After the feast the tribal chief presented them with gifts and their own tent.

When the winter months ended and the full moon showed its glow, Hannah gave birth to a little boy. When the moon came up the night of his birth, in the true African tradition she had Little Two Shoes stand on the highest peak of the tribal camp and raise their son high above his head and offer him long life and freedom before their God. Hannah beamed with delight as she rejoiced at the celebration of her first-born, true African of Native American descent, Scipio Two Shoes.

Although my essay was based on oral history and a fable of sorts, I am proud of my African American and Native American heritage. For instance I was proud when, in 1983, the Mashantucket Pequots won federal recognition. In 1992 they opened Connecticut's first casino, Foxwoods, one of the largest casinos in the world, as well as a first-class museum and research center, and a world-wide educational center. I've known the struggles, hardships, and devastations of some of these tribal members who lived in the Hartford area, as well as that of other tribes. To ride to Ledyard, Connecticut, and to see these magnificent structures, as well as the renewed Reservation, stands as a true tribute to their long years of struggle to gain recognition as the original Native Americans. The Mohigan Tribe followed with a second casino in the same area, opening the Mohegan Sun Casino in 1996.

CHAPTER 5

From My Father's Roots

LITTLE OF THE past history of my father is known. I do know that he had brothers, one of whom I was named after, none of whom I had ever met.

Henry Marshall Milner, my father, who was known only as Marshall Milner, migrated from Griffin, Georgia to Illinois. There he joined the army. Traveling from Illinois to Massachusetts, he dropped in at the "Colored" USO on Main Street in Hartford, where sisters Florence and Grace Stewart served as hostesses. Grace was the oldest and also the shyest and Henry Marshall took a liking toward her. She was not a dancer, so they sat with soft drinks and exchanged addresses. Evidently, it was love at first sight. They kept in touch throughout his military service. Henry was discharged from the army in 1919 and became a Master Mason in Illinois in 1921.

Shortly after he returned to Hartford Henry married his sweetheart, Grace. Out of that marriage came the Milner clan: Marshall, Stanton, Albert, Nelson, Gary, Shirley, and me; twin daughters, who would have been next to the oldest, died shortly after their birth. My dad's mother, Elizabeth Milner, or Grandma Milner, moved to Hartford and lived close by.

Author at age 8, author/mother, father

My dad, my mother, and maternal grandmother were amongst the founding members of the Metropolitan AME Zion Church in Hartford. Dad was also a trustee. He was also one of the first Black entrepreneurs on Albany Avenue, owner of *Milner's SONY Station, Starting & Igniting*. Due to the effects of the first World War, my father entered the Veterans Hospital when I was three years old and remained there until his death.

Maternal Grandmother Florence Stewart

I was twelve by that time. My mother, like many other mothers in our community, worked as a domestic in West Hartford, scrubbing floors on her hands and knees in kitchens where she was not allowed to eat; she had to go out to the back porch to eat her lunch. This was not in the deep south but West Hartford, Connecticut!

I guess my thirst for equality and civil rights can be dated back to the time when, one day, my older brother drove out to pick up my mother and sent me to the door to get her. I must have been around fourteen, and the little girl who answered the door must have been around six. Having grown up with strict respect for my elders, I asked if Mrs. Milner was there. She said, "Oh, you must mean Gracie."

"No, I mean Mrs. Milner and you'd better not call her Gracie again," I replied. She ran back into the house and came back with her mother to whom I repeated that I was there to pick up Mrs. Milner. My mother was summoned to the door and we left.

My mother, who would not dare let any of us disrespect our elders, simply stated, "That's just the way they are." That stuck with me and I became determined not to settle for "just the way they are."

I first emerged into this world at Hartford's Municipal Hospital, around midnight on October 29, 1933. My family had moved from the south end of Hartford and was living in the north end on Main Street, across from our church, Metropolitan AME Zion, which owned a two family house next to the church parsonage. The parsonage is now the church office and my birth home is still standing but under new ownership.

As the youngest of six boys, with one younger sister, I soon became the "hand-me-down kid." Except for my new Easter outfits, all I wore were hand-me-downs from my older brothers. I wore patched pants and torn dungarees long before they became designer jeans. I wore knickers—those pants that bagged at the knees—before I grew into long pants.

My old neighborhoods housed the Black "who's Who" of north Hartford. On Capen Street there were the Milner boys and the Strong girls, as well as the Footes, Duvals, Jacksons, Joneses, Douglases, and many more. My dentist, Dr. Dixon, and my family physicians, Dr. Warren and Dr. Jackson, were on Main Street. Johnson's and L. B. Barnes Funeral Homes were also on Main Street. Back then they were called "colored" funeral homes. During this period of my life African Americans had gone from being called "Negro" to "colored." Although ownership has changed from Jewish to African American, the old grocery store that I used to go to in the 30's, on the corner of Capen and Barbour Street, still remains.

On Wooster Street we lived around the corner from Doc Hurley, who has become a Hartford sports legend, as well as George Howard, the Plummers, and the Alexanders, all of whom lived on Suffield Street. Across the street from us were the Worthams, Rose and Pat Muse, and

Billy Lynch, who became a noted boxer. Patsy and Bootsy Coleman also lived on Wooster Street, along with Charlie Daniels, Clyde Billington, The Clouds, Jenkins, and Smiths.

Hartford's largest Black family, the Gardners, lived next to the synagogue, which is now the Mount Olive Baptist Church, on Suffield Street. Ella Brown, Hartford's first African American policewoman, lived behind us on Main Street, above Lincoln Dairy, our local ice cream parlor. She, along with Madison Bolden, became the most feared, but respected, detectives to us neighborhood kids. Behind me, also on Main Street, were the Independent Social Center, the Black boys and girls club, social service, recreation, and job training center for our neighborhood. This organization also ran Camp Bennett. Sam Jenkins, the director, Frank Simpson, and Don Summers ran the center. These men were all mentoring fathers of our neighborhood.

Fortunately, most of the kids from my neighborhood were at Camp Bennett when the worst circus fire in America took place, right on Barbour Street. Had we been home we would have been at the circus. In fact we cried and begged until our mother promised to take us to the circus when we returned home. Huger Lee, the wife-to-be of my oldest brother, Marshall, would have been at the circus as well except for some last minute change. Upon hearing of the raging fire, her older sister jumped into her car and drove immediately to Hartford from Waterbury in a panic, praying all the way, only to find her sister safe.

I ended up moving to Camp Bennett after my freshman year at Hartford Public High School. I moved in with the caretakers of the camp, the Scotts, and attended Glastonbury High School, becoming the only "brown" student. That was the name given to me by a few of my close friends, but not out of disrespect; to them I became their "brown friend."

I entered the Army Reserves while in high school and then the U. S. Air Force, eventually going to Mobile, Alabama, where I first met "Jim Crow" and all of his buddies—the "For White Only" signs, the back window "For Colored Only" where I could only get leftover, take-out food from white restaurants, the segregated buses, etc. This was a lifestyle I was not used to and could not, and would not, adjust to.

I married Mary Rogers, a Hartford native, while in the Air Force. I was only nineteen at the time and married over the objections of my mother and most of my family members. In fact, I spent my honeymoon in the Bellevue Square housing project where she lived with her grandmother. After my marriage and the many racial injustices I faced while stationed in Alabama after my discharge, I couldn't get back to Hartford fast enough. Sadly Hartford also had segregation, not by law but by design: No Blacks above the ranks of cleaning people or elevator operators in department stores, banks, or insurance companies, quota systems for Blacks in public housing and housing "redlining" throughout the city where no Blacks were allowed to rent or to buy. Just around that time a young, seventeen-year-old, angered by racism, moved to Hartford from the south, by the name of Wilber Gene Smith.

CHAPTER 6

Wilber Gene Smith, An Era of Civil Rights

WHEN WILBER G. SMITH arrived on the scene from the south, the 1950's civil rights movement was just getting underway. Angry from the racism that he and his family faced in the south, he soon found that racism was alive and well "up south" as well. It didn't take him long to join the fight against the injustices from which he thought he had fled.

I first met Wilber shortly after his arrival; I had entered the U. S. Air Force and was home on leave. He had just become involved with the local branch of the National *Association for the Advancement of Colored People* (NAACP) and was lecturing a group of young men and women at the Independent Social Center on Main Street about the need to get involved. When I returned to Hartford after my discharge, Wilber had become even more active with the NAACP and headed its youth group. By that time the south was in the early stages of a civil rights war. There had been lynchings, burnings, demonstrations, and violent racial activity throughout the south. Rosa Lee Parks had refused to go to the back of the bus and a young minister from Atlanta by the name of Martin Luther King, Jr., had agreed to lead a bus boycott in Montgomery, Alabama where he had become pastor of his first church.

State Senator Wilber G. Smith

The Rev. Richard Battles, a leader in the *Southern Christian Leadership Conference* (SCLC), had just moved to Hartford to pastor the Mount Olive Baptist Church. SCLC was a civil rights organization composed mainly of religious leaders and followers. Wilber Smith, Shirley Scott, Raymond Blanks, Carrie Perry, myself, and others had come together to organize the Hartford chapter of the *Congress On Racial Equality* (CORE), which at that time was a more militant national civil rights organization. Our aim was to get directly involved in the civil rights movement.

After several strategy sessions we decided to meet with Rev. Battles for advice and direction. Out of that first meeting, in the basement of Mount Olive, it was decided that we would unite our forces and take a trip south to support the movement. Our plan was to join Rev. Dr. King in his demonstrations. After several meetings we decided, as other groups across the nation had done, to find a sponsor to charter a bus and go south for a weekend of direct involvement in the civil rights demonstrations that were taking place. That next week we experienced anxiety, fear, and hope as we prepared to head south.

It was a quiet evening when approximately a hundred people gathered in front of the Mount Olive Baptist Church to see close to twenty of us off. There was much tension and prayer; we had received news that three buses were attacked and burned, some people were beaten near Albany, Georgia, our destination, and Rev. Dr. King was still in jail. This gave us more the reason to go to Albany and join with those who were present at his release and demonstrating against racial injustices. There were many who pleaded with us not to go, but after much prayer and determination we began to board the bus. Janet Pitts, a local gospel singer who was pregnant at the time, boarded the bus in tears as her family pleaded with her not to go. Another local gospel singer, Eleanor Green, also boarded and once we began to travel the two of them led us in singing Negro spirituals and gospel songs.

With the leadership of the late Rev. Richard Battles we got underway. Raymond Blanks, Wilber G. Smith, and I were appointed bus monitors; we were assigned to keep calm and direction throughout the trip. During most of the journey we sang, talked, prayed, and tried to sleep. The trip itself was uneventful.

We were joined by a bus out of New York City and made our way to Albany. There were those who waved us on along with others who gave us negative hand signals. Our only real confrontation during the trip was in a small southern town where we stopped at a restaurant in the wee hours of the morning. Both of our buses were integrated and we just piled out and headed toward the door. We were stopped by the janitor, who happened to be an elderly Black man. He asked us "where do ya'll think you're going" and began to direct us to a window on the side of the restaurant when his White boss came to the door. Evidently he saw dollars: his restaurant was empty at that time of the morning and he said, "Let them through, they're from out of town. Let's feed them and let them get on their way." We ate without further confrontation, then continued on our way.

As we neared the border of Albany, we were joined by two patrol cars from the Georgia State Police. Because of what happened with the buses before us and with the state police just watching, we became a little nervous as one car drove in the lead and the other one positioned itself behind us. It seemed forever before we drove up to a church and was greeted by a friendly crowd, cheering, shouting, and just about dancing in the streets. We thought that all of this was just for us until we found out that the Rev. Dr. Martin Luther King, Jr. had just been released from jail and was on his way to this very church. We too became jubilant as we were ushered into the choir stand as "special guests."

We joined in the singing of freedom songs only to be interrupted by an outpouring of cheers as Rev. Dr. King came through the doors and was ushered to the pulpit. He was unshaven, without a tie, but a welcomed sight. As I mentioned earlier, we had come to join those who were demonstrating against his imprisonment as well as to demonstrate against the racial injustices. He immediately began addressing the crowd with his great, strong, oratory voice, even thanking us from coming from "up north" to join in the struggle.

After his speech, his preaching, and some more singing we joined him for a true soul food dinner in the church basement and were then assigned to individual families for overnight housing. Each house was guarded by an individual with a loaded shotgun. This, in itself, left us a bit nervous but we had an uneventful night and headed back to the church in the morning for breakfast and our "marching orders."

It was during this time that I met two young members of the *Student Non-Violent Coordinating Committee* (SNCC), Jesse Jackson and Andy Young. They served as coordinators (young Turks as they were called) giving instructions on non-violent demonstrations and assigning us to "protest locations." I was assigned to join the protest at the Albany downtown public library, which did not allow Blacks to enter. Others went to lunch counters, department stores, City Hall, and other places. We were not fearless. Although I would not admit it then, I was scared but became inspired by the determination of the local residents of all ages, who were putting their lives and jobs on the line. These were the ones who had to live there after we were back in the safety of our homes "up north." Most of the real nasty remarks were made to the Whites who had joined us. We ducked a few stones, bottles, eggs, and tomatoes but, considering what happened to others who had protested, we returned back to Hartford safely.

We returned home determined to continue the struggle, not in the south but here at home. A group of us from the local *Congress On Racial Equality* (CORE), the *Southern Christian Leadership Conference* (SCLC), the *Student Non-Violent Coordinating Committee* (SNCC) and Hartford's *North End Community Action Group* (NECAP) organized civil rights demonstrations against racism in Hartford. We targeted the Hartford Housing Authority, which had quotas as to how many Blacks were allowed to live in public housing, the insurance companies, banks, and two of the major department stores, G. Fox & Company and Brown Thompson's, none of which would hire Blacks above the level of service employees.

Although most of us were considered "young civil rights turks" in our day, we also had our elders who were already addressing the injustices in their own way. Among them were Sam Jenkins, Tom Parrish, Boce Barlow, Frank Simpson, Philmore Troutman, and Russell Cromwell. As young turks we took the struggle to the streets and through our protests and the negotiations of our elders some of the barriers began to crumble. For instance public housing adopted non-discriminatory open housing policies, and both department stores changed their policies, along with insurance companies and banks. However, this did not end racism, injustice, or our ongoing struggle.

My relationship with Rev. Dr. King and Jesse Jackson, who became a minister, was to continue. I joined them in Bessemer and Montgomery, Alabama, participated in the historic March On Washington, linked arms with them at various visits to the nation's capitol, as well as Rev. King's and Jackson's visits to Hartford, Connecticut.

CHAPTER 7

The March That Moved and Changed a Nation

EARLY IN THE wee hours on the morning of August 28, 1963, close to one hundred greater Hartford residents boarded a train that originated in Springfield, Massachusetts and headed for Washington, D.C. Like the Springfield passengers we represented a multi-ethnic group of people and organizations including the NAACP, CORE, SNCC, NECAP, SCLC, the Urban League, the Ministerial Alliance, unions, and just plain folk who were sick and tired of being sick and tired. We boarded with our walking shoes, thermos of coffee and/or cocoa and a variety of foods. Many carried placards designating their organizations. On our way toward Washington we stopped in New Haven, Bridgeport, Stamford, New York, New Jersey, Delaware, and Maryland as more marchers boarded. Amtrak had put on a special train and we dubbed it "The Freedom Train." As our train headed past highways we could see buses, vans, and cars on the highways loaded with people headed toward our nation's capitol.

Although the march will always be remembered most for the great "I Have a Dream" speech given by the late Rev. Dr. Martin Luther King, Jr., many of this nation's leaders were also organizing and leading the march. Among them were A. Phillip Randolph, Baynard Rustin,

Cleaveland Robinson, Walter Ruether, Roy Wilkins, Dorothy Height, John Lewis, Whitney Young, James Forman, Jesse Jackson, and Andy Young. They were joined by hundreds of other religious, community, political, and social service leaders.

When we finally headed for the Lincoln Memorial Monument we became a part of a sea of human flesh. Traffic was at a standstill, except for the hundreds of cars and buses that were being directed to their parking places. By the time the march began, the crowd was estimated at 250,000 people of all ages, races, and economic status, marching hand in hand, arm in arm, heading toward the Washington Monument to the Lincoln Memorial and singing with jubilation, yet our minds were set on the seriousness of our cause.

A. Phillip Randolph, leader of the Planning Team, had given the march the theme "A March for Jobs and Freedom" and many of the banners carried that theme.

It was close to 1:00 P.M. when we arrived at the Lincoln Monument. The day was hot and even more so with thousands of bodies pushing to get as close to the speaker's platform as possible, which was on the stairs at the foot of the Lincoln Memorial Monument. There were many speeches, songs, and recitations, but around 3:00 P.M., as some were beginning to tire from standing and the heat, the great Mahalia Jackson took the microphone and began her version of the song "I've Been Bucked and I've Been Scorned." That cooled the crowd in their tracks. From where I stood on a small hill near the platform, I could see nothing but a sea of bodies swaying and waving to the words sung by Mahalia. This was a beautiful sight to behold. Her inspirational singing provided a great prelude for the introduction of the Rev. Dr. Martin Luther King, Jr., who was the next and final speaker.

As Dr. King Jr., was introduced, the crowd grew respectfully silent, then thunderous applause followed as he approached the podium. He started his great speech slowly, but by the time he reached the part where he stated that "America has given the Negro a bad check; we are here today to redeem that check," the crowd was roaring, chanting, clapping, crying, and hanging on each and every word. When he ended with the words from an old Negro Spiritual, "Free at last, free at last, great God Almighty, we are free at last," the crowd broke loose with what I am sure was the greatest sound of applause and amens that Washington, D.C. had ever heard! August 28, 1963 will always be one of the greatest days in American history.

Months after returning from the March on Washington, I decided to move back to the "Big Apple," New York City, where I had previously spent three years. During my first stay I had taken courses through New York University and became a Junior Pharmacist at the District 65 Union Pharmacy, at the union headquarters. Cleveland "Cleve" Robinson was then head of the union and was often visited by his close friend Rev. Dr. Martin Luther King, Jr. It was at the union that I had another opportunity to speak to Rev. Dr. King, the day before he was stabbed by a woman, while signing autographs for his new book.

After returning to New York I faced one of my darkest days when I came out of the Subway Station at Times Square, in Manhattan. Traffic had come to a halt, and everyone was staring at the moving sign that announces "Happy New Year" every year, as the ball drops down just above it. But that afternoon of April 4, 1968, the sign had another message: "Rev. Dr. Martin Luther King, Jr. had been shot in Memphis." Like most others in the crowd I stood there for what must have been a half an hour, but it seemed like hours. Soon after, the sign read "Rev. Dr. King is dead." Somehow, simultaneously, many of us began to sing and mumble through our tears "We Shall Overcome." At that moment, not only those of us at Times Square, but the entire world stood still.

New York City gave me the opportunity to stay active in the civil rights movement. Although I never became active with the group, I often attended meetings of the Black Panthers who, until this day, I firmly believe played a positive role in America's civil rights struggle. During that time I also met and had an audience with the Honorable Elijah Mohammed, as well as Malcolm X, who would address crowds at the corner of Lenox Avenue and 125th Street, in Harlem. I became such a regular that when the Muslim brothers spotted me they would bring me closer to the front of the podium. It was at that time that Malcolm X first invited me to attend the Mosque on 116th Street, which I did on several occasions. After Malcolm X's assassination, my now deceased cousin, Chester Sparks, who was one of the Funeral Directors of the Unity Funeral Chapel on 8th Avenue in Harlem, directed his funeral.

On the social side of my New York stay, I had the opportunity to meet with and visit the homes of singers Dinah Washington, Sarah Vaughn, Little Jimmy Scott, Billie Holiday, and Jonathan Brice, as well as writer James Baldwin and others. Although they were celebrities, off stage and out of the sight of the media, they were just plain folk and good company.

I left my pursuit to become a pharmacist at District 65 Pharmacy, and became more active in the community by taking a position as an Executive Assistant to the Chairman, David Billings, of the New York Council Against Poverty, New York City's answer to the Community Renewal Team of Greater Hartford. That led me to an appointment as an Assistant Deputy Commissioner for Community Development, by then Mayor Lindsay, under newly appointed Deputy Commissioner David Billings. My primary responsibility was overseeing staff and working with some of New York's toughest youth gangs. Working productively with these gangs and seeing the positive outcomes of my involvement was one of my most rewarding experiences while living in New York City.

CHAPTER 8

A Hartford Childhood

IN 1984, WHILE serving as mayor of the city of Hartford, I wrote an article for the *Northeast Magazine* of the *Hartford Courant* newspaper that dealt with memoirs of my childhood days. I have included portions of this article that focus on my early days in Hartford:

During the 1983 flood I stood atop a dike on the Connecticut River watching the sandbagging operations of our city employees. It was a race against time as they piled the hundred-pound sacks of sand against the stack of railroad ties that served as a temporary dike at the railroad crossing. I gave a deep sigh of relief, for they were winning the fight against the muddied waters brought by two weeks of heavy rain that was continuing to rise and threatening to cross onto a city street. As I stood there, I recalled the headlines of the *Hartford Courant* on March 19, 1936: "City Ravaged by Greatest Flood, Bridge Over Connecticut River Closed." I was a mere tyke then, about 2 ½-years-old. I was too young to understand, but not too young to remember my whole family joining the crowds to watch as the waters flooded Riverside Park, came up North Pleasant Street, Morgan and State Streets and turned Bushnell Park into a lake.

Many years and events had passed between the flood of '36 and the flood of '83. As I watched the river angrily flapping against the dikes that now protect our city, I reminisced about my own life in Hartford, about the good old days and days not so good. My mind flashed back to my childhood. It was just one year after the flood that my dad was hospitalized due to the effects of being a soldier in what was called the first, or Great World War. Ten years later he died, never returning home. To me he was a giant, one of the first Blacks to have his own auto repair shop in Hartford, originally on the corner of State and Commerce Streets, and later on Albany Avenue.

Albany Avenue has always been a somewhat strange street. It runs about three miles from Main Street out to West Hartford. The poor, whether Italians, Black, or Puerto Rican, were always located at the east end; the middle class located in the middle, spreading out to the Blue Hills area; and Hartford's wealthiest families settled on the upper end and several streets bordering West Hartford.

Before being hospitalized, my dad had provided us with a second floor flat on Capen Street, near the corner of Barbour, which we shared with my great grandmother, Abigail, and my Aunt Flossie. There were eleven of us in a seven room flat. Those were the days of trolley cars, Wonder Bread at five cents a loaf, and a handful of jelly beans for a penny. For me, the youngest of six boys, those also were the days of hand-me-downs, patched pants, and elbow-worn coats with holes in the pockets. Knickers were in style then. I was more embarrassed because of my skinny legs and my long socks that would never stay up in spite of the rubber bands, than I was about the patches of mixed colors that covered the torn spots in my long pants handed down by my brothers. Most of the kids in my neighborhood wore patches on their pants too.

During that period the, so-called "War On Poverty" had not begun. Everyone around us was poor. No one had television to portray the good life to us. That probably helped prevent us from becoming negative about our impoverished living conditions. Instead, we were fascinated by the tales my mother told of the rich folks she worked for in West Hartford.

Most of our other news came by radio. We would get the Sunday paper, but only concentrated on the comics. Little Orphan Annie and Dick Tracy were around then, wearing the same clothes and never aging. Our favorite pastime, after church on Sundays, was tuning the radio to "The Green Hornet" and "The Shadow," two mystery story series. As the radio voice asked, "Who knows what evil lurks in the hearts of men?" one of my older brothers would switch off the light, throwing us all into a moment of fright.

Most of our after-school activities, besides homework and housework, centered around the church and the neighbors. On Capen Street we lived across from the Joneses and down from the Strongs. The Strong family provided ideal playmates; they had a large number of girls and we were mostly boys. We were too young to court, but not too young to flirt; we batted our eyes, winked, wrote our names and drew hearts in the dirt and on trees, or we etched our initials, and sometimes we even dared to hold hands and giggle. Their backyard was our playground. Big brothers, Norman and Ed Strong, were always on hand to act as chaperones as we played hide-and-seek with Gladys, Christine, Dorothy, and Barbara. My older brothers Marshall and Stanton had graduated to the courting stage and kept themselves too busy to tattletale on us. Through Gloria Johnson's geological research, we later learned that we were distant cousins. They, too, were descendants of the Caples family.

We spent a lot of weekends walking up Capen Street to Keney Park, a few blocks away. In the summertime we would play in the playground or fish in the pond. In the winter we would ice skate and find warmth and hot chocolate waiting for us in the Pond House. Keney Park was our "country club" with its sprawling acres of tall trees where we could play cowboys and Indians, or swing and climb in the playground. It also was the family picnic place where grandmother, mother, aunt, cousins, sister, and all of my brothers and I would go. We'd spread out our blanket or worn sheet and enjoy our milk, peanut butter and jelly, and an occasional ham spread sandwich. There would always be an extra treat like home-baked cakes and cookies.

Moving from Capen Street to Wooster Street was both exciting and tearful, as we said goodbye to our playmates and wondered what the Arsenal School on Main Street would be like, and if we would be allowed to cross Main Street and go to Keney Park. I must have been 8 or 9-years-old at the time. Wooster Street was like a paradise to me. We not only had a second floor flat, but an attic in a house owned by the Independent Social Center. The attic became our bedrooms for the boys and our play area.

It was another poor neighborhood, but we had our own outdoor playground as well, with swings and all, right in our own backyard. The playground was built behind the Social Center's property on Main and Suffield Streets and ours on Wooster Street. Also behind our house was Lincoln Dairy, the ice cream parlor where we could get a big cone for a nickel.

Our church, Metropolitan AME Zion, where it seemed we spent all day Sunday, was also across Main Street. Sunday School followed Sunday breakfast, then church, home for dinner, and back to church for "Buds of Promise." We had to leave together, and return home together: we were family.

In those days, our family doctors, Dr. Jackson and Dr. Warren, would make house calls, even though their offices were within walking distance. Everyone went to their front windows when the doctor's car pulled up to one of our houses.

Wooster Street offered us the best of times and the worst of times. While we were on Wooster Street, my father and my Grandmother Stewart, the disciplinarian of the family, died. Grandmother Stewart was my mother's mother, a strong Hartford native, not only in faith, but in using her hand instead of a switch, razor strap, or belt when discipline was forthcoming. None of my elders believed in whipping clothes; they would make us strip to our bare buttocks. I guess they figured that if they hit us where we sat down, we would straighten up.

It worked. Grandmother Stewart also carried with her the fear of and belief in God, but instilled in me the fear of lightning. When she heard a thunderstorm approaching, she would order us to sit quietly on the back porch with her and "watch God at work" as she called it. I try my best to be inside when it is lightning, and let God do His work outdoors, even to this day.

Another fearful woman on my block was Policewoman Ella Brown, Hartford's first policewoman of color. She lived directly behind us over the ice cream parlor. She was big and could be mean looking, but she was the kindest woman on the block; but when she spoke, we listened. With Ella Brown around my mother had nothing to worry about leaving us at home while she worked all day. Her fence was the only one in the neighborhood that we dared not climb over. We would take turns ringing her doorbell to ask her permission to fetch the ball that often went into her yard as we played catch. We were always able to retrieve the ball, and often a handful of cherries from her trees, but not without a lesson in good citizenship and manners. We would look hungrily at her small tree that always had an abundance of cherries, but we dared not climb over and raid it.

Taking turns to fetch the baseball was no problem because there were a bunch of kids on our block: the Worthams, Joneses, Smiths, Williamses, Daniels, Lynches on my end of Wooster Street; the Plummers, Lewises, Gardiners, and Hurleys on Suffield Street; the Kings on Main Street; Jacksons on Bellevue Street and many more. It was our gang. At the other end of Wooster, at Pavilion, lived the Billingtons, Clouds, Paramores, and other families we thought were well-to-do. They actually were the working poor of today and the middle class of my younger days.

Bellevue Square, a public housing development that, at the time, was heralded as a model for the nation and where many of Hartford's upcoming African Americans moved to, did not exist while I was growing up. Bellevue Street and Village Street were just pathways, tree-lined streets that linked us to the footbridge on West Avon Street and across to Riverside Park. Back then, unlike at Keney Park, we could go to

Riverside Park and take a sneak swim in the dirty Connecticut River or the new Palotti Pool.

One of our joys in those days was waiting for the iceman to come along on his worn out horse drawn wagon. As he chopped the large ice blocks into sizes to fit our iceboxes, chips of ice would be left behind. As soon as we knew that he was on his way up the stairs, we would raid the ice wagon for those precious pieces of frozen water before they melted away. Vendors with horse drawn wagons were familiar sights in our neighborhood. There were the ragman picking up coal sacks of clothing too ragged to reuse, the fish man, and the vegetable and fruit man. Each barked out his trade, stopped to barter and to hang the bag of feed around his horse's neck.

In those days, no one would bother the horses or poke fun at the peddlers. The horses were old, worn out, sway backed, and slow moving creatures with blinders. We did sometimes poke fun at the vendors, but not if we saw a curtain pulled back or a window go up. Every mother who looked out of a window was your mother, as far as discipline was concerned. Punishment was shared. The unwritten code was to respect all of our elders. Those who would be considered the neighborhood drunks or "crazies" were oftentimes our best protectors from the neighborhood bullies.

Weekends in early Hartford were exciting. On Saturday mornings we hurried to get our chores done so that we could earn ten cents and head for the Daly Theatre, past the Tunnel (the intersection of Albany Avenue and Main Street). All seven of us had assigned chores, rotating each Saturday. The chores became more complex as we got older, from sweeping sidewalks, stairs, washing dishes, ironing, to polishing furniture or dusting. Each of us, except for our younger sister, learned how to and had to prepare the evening meal.

As the youngest of the boys, I was always stuck with holding my sister's hand as we walked to our favorite weekend event, the movie theater. Our first stop along the way would be the grocery outlet, next to the Barnard School, for a pound of long, thin salted pretzels for a nickel. We each brought our own, or bartered with each other, trading pretzels for popcorn or candy. The nickel we spent to see the show was well worth it. There were two full-length features and one to-be-continued, several cartoons, the news, special events, and previews of coming attractions.

We were always home before dark and in time to sit down for supper promptly at 6:00. This was a daily routine, except for Sunday. Sunday was the big meal of the week and was served around 4:00, with dessert around 6:00. My Sunday favorite was the large smoked ham with potato salad, homemade biscuits, mother's own special recipe for baked beans, and iced tea. Each meal usually began and ended with a short argument about whose turn it was to set the table, say grace, or wash or wipe the dishes. In our house, arguments were always short-lived; Mother had the last word. None of us would dare talk back to or argue with her.

Many of the summers of my youth were spent at Camp Courant, a day camp, where we would take the bus from in front of the Barnard Brown School and ride to the camp in Farmington, Connecticut. My best summers were spent at Camp Bennett in South Glastonbury, Connecticut. Camp Bennett was located on 142 acres of prime rural country tucked away at the bottom of a steep hill. Owned by the Independent Social Center, it was a camp for disadvantaged youth from as far away as Florida, and had been founded at a time when the Hartford YMCA refused membership for Black youths.

Mr. Samuel Jenkins was the director of both the center and the camp. He and his assistant, Mr. Frank Simpson, provided a father image to many of the youth. Many of Hartford's leaders and doers are alumni of Camp Bennett. The campers included all of the Milner clan (Marshall, Stanton, Albert, Nelson, Gary, Shirley, and myself), Doc Hurley, John "Turk" Cuyler, Cap Perry, Lenny King, John Carter, the Ciceros, Worthams, Hodges, Blanks, Powells, Pertillers, Milliners, Littmans, Pattersons, and the list goes on like the Who's Who of Hartford's original Black families.

If you had been a poor Black youth in Hartford (and most of us were), you'd probably get a chance to spend part of your summer at Camp Bennett. We'd leave Hartford for the thirteen mile trip oftentimes on the back of an open truck loaded with battered suitcases, tied-up boxes, and brown shopping bags that held summer gear for more than 50 boys and girls, some with tears streaking down their faces as parents waved farewell to children leaving on their first trip away from home. I am sure our trips to camp offered some relief to our parents, who never could afford vacations. This way they could relax a little after work while we were away.

Looking back at Camp Bennett, I feel that none of today's conveniences could replace the unpainted wooden cabins with their heavy, flapping, wooden shutters as windows; swimming and fishing in the natural lake; the overnight campouts in the woods; the cookouts; the hikes to the country store, old mill, and apple orchard. The apple orchards were owned by the Varni and Preli families, who allowed us to stuff our stomachs, as well as our pockets, with the best apples and peaches ever. The height of our hikes was sitting on the Varni lawn at dusk watching cartoons and enjoying the treats we bought at the country store. Those were the good old days that cost little but taught me a lot.

Those of us who were old enough spent the rest of the summer picking tobacco on one of the many tobacco fields that surrounded Hartford. We got up early to board old school buses and be driven out to suburban farms. We spent most of the day in the hot, humid sunshine, sliding on our rear-ends up and down long rows, pulling off the long tobacco leaves and piling them in large canvas baskets. Not only was the weather hot and humid and the work hard, but the sap from the tobacco plants left pitch black stains on our hands and clothes. The dry, dusty fields also added to our misery.

Back at home, downtown Hartford was the hub. We lived in an ethnically-segregated community. Downtown was the "melting pot" where the poor of the South End mingled with the poor of the North

End searching for bargains to make ends meet. It was always crowded and alive.

Quincy Market in today's Boston could not compare with the open markets along Front, Market, and State Streets. G. Fox's Toy Department was our Winter Wonderland. You could always find its owner, Beatrice Fox Auerbach, greeting customers as she cuddled her miniature bulldog. Sage Allen, Grant's Five and Ten, and the Poli, Parson, and Strand Theatres were all exciting places for Hartford residents to meet.

The State Theatre on Windsor Street was the Civic Center of that day, where the world's greatest entertainers came to perform. Hartford had its own Cotton Club, the Club Sundown, also on Windsor Street, which provided a stage for some of the top Black entertainers. Bill Savitt, Arthur Godfrey, Willie Pep, Jesse Owens, Ed Sullivan, and young Joe Louis were all household names. Be-bop was in. Even though there were trolley cars, most of us walked to and from downtown; our parents could not afford for us to "waste" money riding, even when we carried heavy bags of groceries.

At the end of my freshman year at Hartford High School I moved to South Glastonbury with the Scotts, caretakers of Camp Bennett, and left behind my own family. The excitement of making a change and living in the country overshadowed the loneliness of not being with my family, to whom I returned some weekends.

Glastonbury was the setting for the beginning of my young adult years. It was there that I met my surrogate mother, Mom Kuszai; her son, Jim, became my new brother. As the only Black at Glastonbury High School, I was known by my classmates as "little brown friend," a term used to show identification and affection. A few years later, after bouts in the armed services and as a civil rights worker, I chuckled at the thought of my color being used affectionately as a positive identification.

I became awestruck that day when I stood watching the Connecticut River peak, as my thoughts wandered back and I pieced together the years between the floods of '36 and '84. How short a span it really had been from that little brown boy with patched, knicker pants to the person I was now, dressed in my three-piece suit and surveying the flood waters as mayor.

Yet, I thought, has Hartford really changed that much? There was still a Milner Auto Shop on Albany Avenue, and until a few weeks ago it was not far from my dad's original shop. The new shop was opened by my brother, Gary. There are some noticeable changes on Albany Avenue; fewer trees and two large supermarkets and the Five and Ten's are now gone. The street is still crowded with people, but the faces have changed from white to black to brown along lower and middle Albany Avenue. The older and wealthier families of Hartford still live on the upper tip of Albany Avenue. And instead of Italian and Jewish shops, there are now Puerto Rican, African American, and West Indian vendors along the Avenue. The street is once again coming alive. Fast food restaurants and a major supermarket are replacing the many shops and stores that were deserted and burned during the riots of the late sixties.

I enjoy riding or walking along Albany Avenue and seeing the new neighbors who stand on the corners, lean out of the windows, or go in and out of the many shops. The people along Albany Avenue were strangers to me in my childhood days, and I feared the many white faces. Today I hear the same cry of fear from many whites who are now strangers to the new ethnic community of Albany Avenue. Little has changed.

My old, battered house on Capen Street, with its first and second floor porches, is now gone, replaced by a bold yellow prefabricated, and not very majestic housing structure. The corner store at Barbour and Capen is still there, as well as the gas station next to the Strong house on Capen, facing Martin Street. Mr. Silver, the Jewish owner of the corner store, has long been dead, and the large picture windows have been replaced with small window openings.

The Barbour Street bus still travels the rout of the old trolley, and in the mornings the buses are still crowded with domestics going out to work in West Hartford. The new riders are the hundreds of students who ride to school, a luxury we weren't afforded in my day.

My mother, sister, grandmother, two brothers, Marshall and Albert, and my Aunt Flossie, along with cousin Chester, are now dead. Although the "switch" and razor strap have gone with my mother, she still reigns as matriarch of our family.

My three remaining brothers and I are still in the Hartford area and we are all grandfathers. It is good to know that the Hartford I enjoyed as a kid has not changed that much for us. None of us have become rich; we still enjoy peanut butter and jelly sandwiches. And many of our relatives still live in public housing and poor neighborhoods.

The "War on Poverty" has not been won. Television has not solved, but added to, the problems of the poor, as it brings the good life directly into the homes of those who are still struggling at the bottom. The stories our parents told about the rich in West Hartford were like fairy tales, but television has brought home the stark reality of the differences between the haves and the have-nots. The negative social impact of this exposure to reality can be measured by the drastic increase in crimes committed by people who are economically disadvantaged.

Keney Park remains a sprawling oasis. The old Pond House has been renovated and the playground has once again come alive with children. It also has its own swimming pool now, and it is once again becoming a place for a family picnic, for family fun.

I now live on the other side of the park, in a house on a street that I dared not walk down in my youth. It was a predominately white neighborhood, and unless you were a domestic on your way to work you did not dare intrude upon the quietness of most neighborhoods outside of north Hartford, if you were a person of color. It was an unwritten law, but one quite often enforced by the owners as well as police. Today my street is ethnically mixed. It is still quiet, but also used by many who go to and from Keney Park. I, too, still enjoy the walk to the park, a shorter walk, but still one that offers me a chance to get away. Keney Park is still my "Country Club."

The Independent Social Center on Main and Suffield Streets has long been torn down and new housing units have been built in its place. The two Jewish Synagogues, one on Suffield and Wooster and the other on Wooster and Pavilion, are now both Black churches. Lincoln Dairy is now across the Street, on Main. The old Arsenal School that I attended as a child has been replaced by the new SAND Everywhere School. The strict discipline and row-seat desks have been replaced by a more open classroom approach.

My church still stands, now opening its doors to fourth and fifth generations of the Milner and Stewart clans. Little has changed, except for the addition of a ramp and elevator installed for the elderly and handicapped.

The downtown theaters are now gone and have been replaced by multi-cinemas in suburban malls, although one has been built on New Park Avenue in Hartford's southend. Our downtown has become a ghost of things past, waiting to be called back to life by developers with vision, who remember the good old days. No longer is it a "melting pot" boiling over with a rich mixture of Hartford's multi-ethnic population. For the most part it has become a pot that boils over in the morning with "ingredients" who come to work in our city during the day, and then empty out at night as they scurry back to their suburban towns.

The heart of our city of yesterday, Windsor Street and those around it, which contained the open market of my childhood, is now cold and boring, with its computer centers, parking lots, and office buildings that have buried the sounds of a happy, busy, exciting neighborhood. However, with the new Science Center, a community college, hotels, and retail stores beginning to open up in that area downtown may once again become a people place.

I watch and listen to our new generation with sadness, as parents shut themselves off from "neighborhood mothers," not allowing adult neighbors to chastise their children. The neighborhood mother is missing from a lot of our educational, religious, and community organizations. Throughout our neighborhoods, fences are built to keep neighborhood children out. Some of our young openly talk back to and poke fun at their elders. Our neighborhood mothers, too, must become a part of Hartford's heralded renaissance.

Camp Bennett is now closed to the disadvantaged youth of our city; thus the good works of many have been lost forever for many of our children of today and tomorrow. The YMCA changed its policy over thirty years ago, and now opens its doors to anyone who can afford to be a member. This still excludes many who now live in my old neighborhoods. Today, with fewer playgrounds and recreational facilities, the youngsters of this group find the streets to be their playgrounds.

The tobacco fields have dwindled. A large segment of the workers are now displaced in our city. They are not trained to enter our insurance, banking, or other nonagricultural industries. Though predominately poor, these displaced workers have enriched our city's social, religious, and cultural amenities. As native Hartford youngsters sought higher wages for picking tobacco, farm owners began transporting Black youths from southern schools, followed by young men from the many Caribbean Islands, and then young Americans from Puerto Rico. These three groups now make up a large portion of Hartford's new generation. We have learned to blend in the old with the new. This has been traditional as new settlers migrate to our city.

In that same sense Hartford has not changed since 1936. Immigrants from just about every nationality have made Hartford their home and have woven their cultures into the multi-cultural fabric of our city. When I think about that and my climb from a welfare child in patched pants at the time of the 1936 flood to a proud, but not rich, mayor surveying the flood waters that threaten the same city in 1983, I smile. I smile because I see in the faces of little boys and girls along Capen Street, Park Street, Franklin Avenue, Albany Avenue, Barbour Street, and throughout the city, as a reflection of myself as a child. I smile, for I see another historic first in those faces—the first Hispanic governor of our state, or Hungarian mayor, or another president of color. I see young people in poverty, but not life-long poverty within our young people.

CHAPTER 9

The Early 70's, as Reported by My Niece, Dalia

DALIA MAY IS the daughter of my brother Gary. For her college class on Racial and Ethnic Issues she wrote an essay titled *Thirman L. Milner, Hartford's Finest*. I offer this tribute to her as my beloved niece, who continued her education and career while being a wife and a mother. The last part of her essay documents memories of my life from the early 1970's to the spring of 1999.

The early 1970's brought a new outlook for Uncle Thirman. He stated that instead of fighting the system he decided to join it to benefit his causes and the movement. It was a hard decision and he often needed the prompting of several people who saw him as becoming something really great for the local community and perhaps the state at large. One of these persons was Wilber Smith.

In the 1960's and most of the 1970's Smith was one of Hartford's most militant Blacks. He was the youngest Black state senator and very outspoken about issues from 1971 to 1977. He had dropped out for two years and was elected again, returning in 1981. He had also been the youngest president of the Hartford Branch of the N.A.A.C.P.

Smith began by encouraging Uncle Thirman to run in 1976 for state representative. None the less, Uncle Thirman lost that first election by three votes and said he would never run again. However, in 1978, Wilber and Ruby Long (a resident of a public housing project, Bowles Park) insisted that he run again because they felt that he could make a difference.

In his first of many political victories, Uncle Thirman won by over 300 votes against Clyde Billington, the incumbent. He remained very active in civil rights and in 1979 was the first to cause a state legislator to be censored. This legislator, Representative Reynolds, had used the derogatory term "nigger" in referring to Blacks. Uncle Thirman had originally submitted a bill to have Reynolds kicked out of office but got no support, not even from Black legislators. He made a very passionate effort to then State Treasurer, Henry "Hank" Parker and Senator Wilber Smith, to come to the floor of the House of Representatives and demand support of the Black State Representatives. They finally gave support for a bill to censor that was passed.

In 1980, Jim Monroe, a local businessman, asked if Uncle Thirman would run for mayor. He declined at first; no other Black person, except for an unsuccessful run by Wilber Smith, had ever run for mayor in the state of Connecticut, let alone a capital city, nor in New England. However, there was one Black mayor in New London, Connecticut, at that time but he had been appointed by the town's City Council, not elected by the people. With the insistence of all of those who had prompted him before, he finally decided, why not. "Why Not Milner For Mayor" became his campaign slogan. Although under Hartford's form of government the mayor had no vote, he did have veto power, could impact legislation, city direction, influence business, and serve as a role model to city youth.

During the September Democratic Primary Election of 1981 Uncle Thirman lost by 94 votes to then Mayor George Athanson. Through an investigation by his campaign workers it was found that some absentee ballots had been forged for Athanson's side for persons in convalescent homes and hospitals who were too sickly to sign an absentee ballot or to give consent. It was hard to find a lawyer who would take this case to court, but two days before limitations deadline a young, White lawyer, Attorney Beider of Bridgeport, took the case pro-bono. Attorney Beider was also active in the Civil Rights Movement.

As if things could not get anymore discouraging, it was even harder to find a judge would preside over the case. Six hours before the deadline, a retiring judge took over the case at the last minute. The case became known as "Thirman L. Milner vs. City of Hartford and the Democratic Party." On the third day of the trial the judge told city officials to either agree to a new election or continue with the case and face the consequences of the possibility of someone being jailed and fined for forgery, among other incriminations. The city agreed, as well as Uncle Thirman. For the first time in the state's history a new Democratic Primary Election was set for October 13, 1981.

The day had finally arrived for the new primary election. The tension in the air was thick but everyone sensed victory was close at hand. Several of Uncle Thirman's colleagues from the State General Assembly showed up to help with the campaign. Van loads of people also poured into Hartford to work in his campaign. It is estimated that at least 100 people had come from out of town to assist on the campaign, including a van load from Albany, New York, some from Massachusetts, and state legislators from New Haven, Waterbury, and Bridgeport, Connecticut. Some canvassed the city to do last minute registrations, while others actually pulled folks from their homes, taking them to vote. Rides were offered to and from voting polls. If someone was cooking, there was someone from the campaign to come in and watch the pots. If they could not leave because they had to be with their children someone would come in and baby-sit. If someone had to go to the store a campaign worker would do that too, before taking them to the polls to vote; anything to free Hartford residents to come out and to vote. In all, over 1,000 people assisted Uncle Thirman on his second primary election mayoral campaign.

On October 13, 1981, at about 9:30 P.M., Uncle Thirman claimed victory. He had won the primary by a landslide. Not only in the North End of Hartford, where he had heavy support of African-Americans and West Indians, but all over Hartford. This proved that the "people" believed in his campaign. They finally realized that he was a man for his community.

As an assistant majority leader of Connecticut's General Assembly, as a state representative, he had fought hard for improved housing, elderly assistance, property tax reform, youth services, education, energy assistance, and law enforcement.

As mayor, Uncle Thirman would continue the fight with one of his top priorities being the development and implementation of housing for the city at large to meet the housing crisis, especially for lower income people. He would also continue to work towards the improvement of Hartford's economic outlook for the neighborhoods as well as the downtown area. Another important issue he tackled was crime. His is a belief of attacking causes of crime, which are high unemployment, substandard living conditions, and inadequate education. He supported the elimination of social promotion of school children and continued to work toward fair property classification and property tax relief through tax reform. He made it clear that he was against tax breaks or deferrals that did not significantly benefit Hartford's residents.

Clearly, the people of Hartford were ready for "Milner as Mayor" because on November 9, 1981, Uncle Thirman was elected the mayor of the capital city of Hartford, Connecticut. He won the general election by an even larger margin than the primary election. The turnout of registered African-American voters, at 90 percent, was the largest in the history of the city of Hartford. Because of its historical impact in the Northeast (and nationwide) he was invited all over the country to speak. Connecticut's Black Historical Society urged him to get a portrait painted and he was written up in various magazines including *Time* and *Newsweek* magazines. The portrait was painted by a local artist, Michael Borders, and now hangs in the Thirman Milner Core Knowledge Academy.

As our discussion of this chapter of his life winds down, Uncle Thirman fondly remembers the hard work and the support of the West Indian Community from the very beginning. He states that his first campaign contributions came from the West Indian Social Club and eight other Caribbean Clubs in Hartford, when Collin Bennett, another of Hartford's great men and former Republican city councilman, passed a hat around for donations. His election went beyond party labels.

After his victory and move into the leadership role as Hartford's mayor, Uncle Thirman became active in the National Conference of Black Mayors, becoming first vice president of the conference. He stated this was an honor as he was the only northern mayor. In 1985 he brought the convention of the National Conference of Black Mayors to Hartford. He recalls that at least eighty mayors were in attendance.

During his three terms as mayor, he traveled throughout the United States and the world visiting different countries including Switzerland, France, Germany, Jamaica, Taiwan, Africa, and Italy. In the 1980's he became a founding member of the World Conference of Mayors, which included members from third world countries and the United States. His journeys to Floridia, Italy and Jamaica afforded Hartford sister cities. In Floridia the people greeted him and the other delegates with a large celebration, including a parade. The town also gave him an honorary chair during the twining ceremonies at which time Hartford became Floridia's sister city. This chair currently sits at City Hall to this day.

After deciding not to run for another term as mayor, two years later, in 1989, the Hartford Board of Education renamed the Vine Street School the *Thirman L Milner Elementary School*. Uncle Thirman stated this was a great honor because they had never named a school after a living person before, which made him kind of nervous. The residents of Hartford had one year to protest this decision if they thought that he did not deserve the honor or that, for any reason, the school should not be renamed. No one came forward and the resolution to rename the school was passed. To this day he goes to the school on a regular basis, considering the more than 400 students his kids.

Additionally, during Uncle Thirman's terms as mayor he became director of government affairs for the Edwards Supermarket chain, which was owned by a company called AHOLD of the Netherlands. He took this extra position because the mayorship, though prestigious, was only chartered as part-time, and at that time paid only $17,500 yearly. Being chartered part-time was quite ironic to Uncle Thirman because he described being mayor as full time work with much overtime but no extra pay. Though he needed to supplement his income with other employment he would not give up his responsibility to the City of Hartford.

During his affiliation with the Edwards Supermarket chain he became a member of the Food Marketing Institute, which consisted mainly of CEO's of many major food chains across the country. He later became their chairman of the government relations committee. He also became a member and the vice chairman of the Connecticut Food Association and a member of the Massachusetts and New York State Food Associations, respectively, as the only African American member in all of these associations. He remained with Edwards after he left the mayor's office until 1994 when, due to chronic effects of an illness, he went on medically recommended full disability.

In 1992, after prompting from his long time friend and mentor, Wilber G. Smith, Uncle Thirman ran for the State Senate. Mr. Smith, a former state senator, had hopes of running for the seat again, but became ill. A week before his death, as he lay in his bed, he again asked Uncle Thirman to run in his place. In 1993, Uncle Thirman beat the incumbent, Frank Barrows, and became a state senator while continuing his employment at the Edwards Supermarket office.

I asked him if this was the normal rise in ranks of a politician and Uncle Thirman stated that there was no particular order. He said that the House of Representatives is the lower house and the State Senate is the upper house. He also remarked that if Barbara Kennelly had stepped down from the U. S. Congress before he became ill, he would have definitely moved on a run for Congress. He had spoken with her on this matter but in 1994 Uncle Thirman was struck with yet more unfortunate news; he was diagnosed with a serious illness. At the end of his term in November 1994, he left Edwards and went on full disability as advised by his doctors, which he remains on to this day. At that time the doctors had given him three to six months to live. There must have been something else in the cards because my uncle still stands today. Almost four and a half years later he still lives by the grace of God.

Today, even with his illness, Uncle Thirman still keeps quite busy as well as having served as a local preacher at the Metropolitan A. M. E. Zion Church, our family's church for decades. His brothers Nelson, Gary, Stanton, and I, are current members. My grandparents, Marshall Milner, Sr. and Grace Milner, were also among the founding members. Uncle Thirman recently gave up writing a weekly column for the local newspaper, *Northend Agents*, something he had been doing for more than 24 years. The name of the column started out as "Wake Up Hartford;" it was later changed to "Wake Up Greater Hartford" due to the large number of readers from surrounding suburbs.

As I concluded my research for this paper I asked Uncle Thirman if he would write a book about his life someday. He stated that many had prompted him to do so, even providing him with tapes and a recorder to begin but that he needed to find time to start it.

In closing I would like to comment on what a great learning experience this has been for me. Not only did it increase my knowledge of my heritage, I also received great insight into someone I thought I had "known" all my life. Before my research began all I knew was that Uncle Thirman was the first popularly elected African-American mayor in all of New England. That was enough to make me proud. When I found out all the details of his life, I realized that he was more than just a "First African-American mayor;" he is also a great man whose struggle for his community began years before his mayorship, and still has not ended.

CHAPTER 10

Fighting the Struggle from Within

I T WAS FOLLOWING the civil rights movement of the 50's and 60's, the assassinations of Malcolm X, Rev. Dr. Martin Luther King, Jr., President John F. Kennedy, and his brother, Robert, that my friend and mentor, Wilber G. Smith, then president of the Connecticut State NAACP Conference of Branches, turned my attention toward a different phase of the ongoing struggle for civil rights justice, and equality. He said "wait a minute; we've been fighting the system for more than twenty years. We are just as much a part of the American system as anyone else. We need to be in a position to make change, not just fight for it." It was then that he met with a small group of us to announce that he was considering running for the Connecticut State Senate in the 2nd Senatorial District. The seat was already held by an African America, Boce Barlow, a noted local attorney.

The feeling among some was that the Black community needed more proactive elected officials. We all knew that this would be an uphill fight. First of all it has always been tough to beat an incumbent, especially of the same political party. Secondly we knew that the question would be raised as to why challenge another person of color? Senator Barlow had been supportive of the civil rights movement but had not been an activist. Wilber's goal was to bring the movement into the system where changes could be implemented through legislation.

No one had to give Wilber the "go signal." The election challenge was on and a door-to-door, grass roots campaign was waged. The major media and so-called elite had given the election to Senator Barlow, the endorsed Democratic candidate, long before the polls closed. No way could a young upstart like Wilber Smith beat a Democratic loyalist in a Democratic Primary Election.

The race was on.

Hartford's powerful Democratic Party machine put all of its efforts out to defeat this young upstart who dared to challenge the party's candidate. Smith appealed to the young, the elderly, and to many of those in public housing as his base of support. His fight for election to the State Senate became a new phase of Hartford's civil rights movement.

Many of us who had been active in the movement threw our support behind Wilber. To the dismay of the Democratic Party loyalist, when the final votes were tallied, Wilber G. Smith became the Democratic candidate-elect for Connecticut's 2nd Senatorial District. That Tuesday night, after the polls were closed, a night of jubilation followed. Never before had any Democrat dared challenge Hartford's powerful Democratic machine, led by Boss Bailey, and won. Wilber easily won the general election in November, then took his fight for justice and equality to Capitol Hill in Hartford. He became a greatly respected state senator as well as feared by some because of his fight and determination for just causes. A young Black leader, he was a force to be reckoned with; he became Senate Chairman of the Planning and Development Committee, a committee that was responsible for the state's land, housing, and development.

Hartford still had a large population of poor, underprivileged, and unemployed residents. During Senator Smith's time in office, the United States Congress proposed Enterprise Zones to be set up in cities across the nation to help distressed communities. Senator Smith immediately saw this as an opportunity for Hartford, especially his constituents in the

2nd Senatorial District. This district took in a large section of Hartford's north end, the area of predominately African Americans with a large segment of under and unemployed. Even before Congress moved on this proposal he began his plans.

Senator Smith contacted the President of the United States as well as members of Connecticut's congressional delegation. They all informed him that the Enterprise Zone was only a concept, a proposal, and had not even come before a Congressional Committee for consideration. He didn't care; Smith wanted to know more about it and traveled to Washington, D. C. to get a draft copy of the proposal, which had not been released as yet. However, he had the proposal in his hands before most of those in Congress had possession. After returning to Hartford and going through the volumes of documents, he became even more determined that the Enterprise Zone legislation must be enacted and that Hartford must become a recipient of one of the designated zones.

Smith pulled together a local Enterprise Zone Committee under the state's Planning & Development Committee. He was determined that Hartford should have an Enterprise Zone and also all of Connecticut's largest cities should have designated zones. He called together leadership, business, and community folk from all of these areas and formed a Task Force. They revised the proposed legislation and began to map out areas of these cities that could qualify under the proposed federal legislation. Hartford and several large Connecticut cities won their designated "Enterprise Zones" due to the determination of Wilber Smith who then became known as the "Father of the Enterprise Zones."

CHAPTER 11

My Entrance into Politics

WHEN I RETURNED to Hartford from New York City, Rev. Dr. King, President Kennedy, and his brother Robert, all had been assassinated. President Lyndon Johnson had enacted legislation ending legal segregation but, unfortunately, injustice, bigotry, and racism in its more deceitful form of "institutional racism" was on the upsurge, especially "up south" in New England. Ralph Ellison had written his book *The Spook Who Sat By the Door* and the term "last hired, first fired" was being felt by many as integration began to create new competition in the workforce, particularly in the teaching profession. Traditionally Black colleges were being threatened as segregated White institutions were being integrated by law.

Upon returning I joined the oldest existing community action agency in our nation, the *Community Renewal Team of Greater Hartford* (CRT). I became one of the assistants to the then Executive Director, James Harris, who later appointed me as Director of Public Relations and Communications for the agency, a position that started my writing hobby. Jim Harris went on to become a State Commissioner responsible for the needs of the poor throughout the entire state. CRT became a springboard for many of us who went from fighting the system to becoming part of the system through the elective process.

I was just into my second year of employment at CRT when Senator Smith approached me about running for State Representative. I had no political ambitions and was quite satisfied with my position at CRT. The 7th Assembly District State Representative seat was, at that time, held by an African American whom I grew up with. However, once again the call was for more proactive leadership, someone from the civil rights movement who would bring the momentum and goals of the movement into the political system to effect positive, and needed, change through legislation.

My first response was "no way;" I enjoyed my work and association with the CRT family team and CRT. It was a rewarding experience with the theme "People Helping People to Help Themselves." However, one Saturday morning Senator Smith called and said, "get dressed; I want you to meet somebody." Saturday was my lazy day, especially Saturday mornings, but Wilber was persistent. "I want you to meet somebody today, now, this morning, get dressed."

I did.

In less than an hour Wilber Smith was at my door and we were on our way to a local public housing complex, Bowles Park. Arriving, we parked, got out, and went to the front door of one of the units. Wilber rang the bell and a tall, African American lady with a stern look on her face answered the door. She was in her bathrobe and had the look of someone to be reckoned with. Then she smiled and introduced herself as Ruby Long and ushered us into her small kitchen. She told us to sit down as she poured coffee at a table already set for three. She quickly prepared grits, eggs, and sausages, dished them out, sat down and gave me the "once over" look.

As I began to enjoy my breakfast, and was just about to put my fork to my mouth she looked me straight in the eye and said, "You are going to run." I almost dropped my fork, because of her tone.

All that I could say was "what?"

"You are going to run: we need you and if Wilber says you are the person then you are going to run."

I looked over at Wilber who had a sheepish grin on his face as he kept eating without saying a word. I tried to explain that I had only come back to Hartford less than two years before, that I was completely satisfied with my position at CRT, and that even though I had been an Assistant Deputy Commissioner in New York City I knew little about politics, especially about holding an elective office. She would have none of it.

"You are going to run. We need you, our community needs you. It's our job to get you elected and we will."

I found my food easier to swallow than her determined words. We ended the breakfast with her final words. "Give yourself a week to think about it and come back for breakfast next Saturday, this same time."

Before I left she told Wilber to take me to see Isabel Blake, on Irving Street. Isabel, who I found to be another strong community advocate, held no punches either. She told me that I *would* run and that she would fully support me. After I left, and blasted Wilber for setting me up, I went back to CRT to ponder my decision, although it had already been made for me. I was really left with no choice but to announce that I was running.

That Monday I met with Jim Harris to let him know of my plans. To him my running was not a wise thing to do. As a community action agency CRT looks to its legislative delegation for support. For one of its employees to challenge one of them was, to him, a no, no. Jim advised me that under the then federal "Hatch Act," an act that prohibited certain political activities by those working in agencies receiving federal funding, I would automatically be forced to resign my position with CRT. I later found out that the Hatch Act did not prohibit me from running for public office.

With no income and no campaign funds I announced my run for State Representative.

It was the spring of 1976 when I first entered my candidacy for State Representative of Hartford's 7th Senatorial District. It was a door-to-door campaign, with me and a few volunteers going door to door, passing out flyers, and speaking at issue forums and community affairs. Having been a community activist, I enjoyed knocking on doors, meeting people, and answering questions.

I entered the Democratic Primary Election in September, 1976, as a newcomer to politics as well as the district, but also as a native son who was known to many in the community. However, when the votes came in, I had lost by three votes—three votes! That was it for me: no more politics. I went back to Jim Harris, hat-in-hand, and was reinstated with a promise never to run again. It had been a great experience but, for me the defeat was the end.

Then came the spring of 1978.

The forces began to gang up on me. Of course, Ruby Long, Isabel Blake, and Senator Smith were back with their "you have to run again, you only lost by three votes" mantra. They had rallied a few more folks together and my phone began to ring, both at home and at CRT with, "Milner you have to run." It was like "run Milner run." Again, I was enjoying my position at CRT. I had become Director of Communications, dealing with the public relations aspect of communications for the agency. Run Milner Run!

You guessed it; I gave in, not entirely because of those who kept prodding me to run, but having been involved in the civil rights movement I knew that true, positive change doesn't come about without proactivism. I did feel that I had something to offer and could make a positive difference if I were elected. The issues were simple: poverty, quality education, jobs, economic empowerment, and economic development; issues that are too well known by those of us who have been, and are, community or civil rights activists. Although I was hesitant, I too held Senator Smith's view that there was a better chance for change by getting into the system where you could impact change, instead of just fighting it. So, it was back to Jim Harris again, but I was able to hold onto my job this time, at least until after the election.

I was finally elected State Representative of Hartford's 7th Assembly District, a District representing some of Hartford's poorest and richest residents. My two terms were both challenging and rewarding. Having been in the civil rights movement and community service, it did not take long to adjust to the role of proposing, supporting, and addressing the needs of those for whom I was elected to represent. The needs were basically the same as those I had advocated for throughout my life—justice, equality, economic empowerment, education, and a better lifestyle for all. The majority of those whom I represented were among the middle class and those living below the poverty level.

During my term Connecticut faced an energy crisis and as a member of the Energy Committee more of my proposed legislation was voted into law than that of any other legislator that year. It was also a time when there was a call for welfare reform. Most of the proposed legislation, especially the Workfare Program, was more punitive than supportive or helpful to those on welfare. As a person coming from a family that was forced to go on welfare because of the hospitalization of my father, I took a strong stand against these punitive proposals. Bringing out my family history surprised some, I guess, because I was highlighted in our local daily newspaper. Fortunately, none of the punitive measures were passed.

Another issue that gave me too much media attention during my terms as State Representative began early one Monday morning, while listening to my radio in February of 1980. The first words I heard were that of a State Legislator, who had answered a news service poll on taxes by writing "No! No income tax; no more taxes; limit spending, put the niggers back to work!" I jumped up: was this real? I just knew that it could not be in Connecticut where there were, and still are, more non-Blacks on welfare than Blacks; but these remarks had come from a fellow State Representative who sat only a few seats from me at the State Capitol, who happened to be a former priest. My immediate reaction was that no one with this blatant racist attitude should be sitting in the Connecticut General Assembly. Immediately I reached for the telephone and called the State Capitol to have a "Proposed Bill of Impeachment" prepared in my name, seeking removal of this legislator.

When I arrived at the Capitol the halls were buzzing over these remarks and the word had gotten around that I had called in to have an impeachment proposal drafted, something unheard of in the Connecticut General Assembly. The media was all over the place and I was quickly summoned to the House of Representatives Democratic leadership office, where I was told that the legislator would be making a public apology. Although his remarks were appalling, deplorable, and a scar on the Legislature, I was informed that a vote to impeach or to expel would not succeed.

This did not change my mind about seeking impeachment. Incidentally, some members of the Legislative Black Caucus disagreed with me, stating that my move for expulsion had put them in an "awkward" position and the apology should be accepted to end the matter. This angered me even more.

Here we were in 1980, thirteen years after the March on Washington, and I was being asked to simply accept an apology for blatant, racist remarks made by an elected official of the State of Connecticut—after marching and demonstrating against the racist attitudes of those whom I never met. I was, however, encouraged when then State Treasurer Henry "Hank" Parker, an African American, walked into the meeting of the Black Caucus, slammed his fist on the table and in one of his rare moments of outward display of anger stated, "What is going on? Here we have the Klu Klux Klan recruiting in Connecticut, we are fighting like hell to end apartheid in South Africa and some of you dare to stand here as Black folk and say that it's okay to make racist remarks like this and just apologize! What is wrong with you guys?"

Ash Wednesday was the day on which the House of Representatives met to hear my motion. Here we were going into one of the most holy of all Christian seasons, and dealing with a former priest for using racial slurs. I found that there was not enough support for my motion to impeach but I refused to accept anything less than a "Vote to Censure" by the entire House of Representatives. This would be the first time that our state lawmakers had taken a formal action against a colleague.

Things were tense. The lawmaker who made the remark stood up and gave his apology over what he called his "human error." After hearing the words of the State Treasurer, members of the Legislative Black Caucus, who had met with the leadership for over an hour prior to the legislative session, agreed to back my motion to censure. Along with the Democratic leadership they co-sponsored my resolution to censure. Emotions were high. Those on both sides of this issue were called bigots and worse. There was a "motion" to remove the word "censure" from the resolution. If that word had been eliminated the resolution would have simply been a slap on the wrist. That motion failed by a vote of 70 to 67. The final vote to censure passed 87 to 50, and history was made with that vote—but at what price?

CHAPTER 12

Why Not Milner for Mayor?

IT WAS DURING my second term as State Representative, in the spring of 1980, that Jim Monroe, then owner of the Oasis Oil Company—where I worked part-time as a Sales Representative to supplement my income—first approached me with the idea of running for mayor in 1981. First of all, I was reluctant to run for State Representative. I had never intended to be what one calls a "career politician." After being elected, my aim was to set my objectives and goals, meet them, and then step aside for someone that had people needs and concerns at heart and could bring fresh ideas for solving some of the ills of our society through the legislative process.

Jim, however, was serious about my running for the mayor's office; we talked about it over and over. Finally, at his urging, I decided to approach some local community leaders just to explore the possibility of a Black man, not just running, but winning. Among those I met with were Wilber Smith, Curtis Robinson, a local business owner, the Rev. A. Roger Williams, pastor of Hartford's Union Baptist Church, and several others.

Wilber had run for mayor a few years earlier and although he was not successful, he planted a seed that we knew someday would bloom.

But was 1981 a realistic year to fertilize the seed he planted and bring it to life? For me it was important that I first find out the feelings of my base, Hartford's Black community.

In exploring the possibility I met with mixed feelings; many thought that the time was not ripe. A Black mayor in Hartford? Forget it! The then president of the Greater Hartford Branch of the NAACP told me that I would be wasting the Black vote; I should run for the City Council and forget about the mayor's race. Others felt strongly that it was worth the try. If I was going to take this step I had to feel confident that I could, and would, win.

I next put together an exploratory committee to do some research. The committee found that there were enough registered Blacks to win if there were a 50 percent voter turnout in my favor and if I could pick up at least 40 percent of the Latino vote and 20 percent of the White vote. These figures were important to me because, unlike a State Representative who represents a district that included Hartford and parts of two surrounding towns, Windsor and Bloomfield, my votes for mayor would come only from Hartford and I needed to know I could win. With that information, and the feelings from many in the community that it was time for a change, I decided to at least put feelers out and do some personal exploring.

I met with the present mayor, our town chairman, our state's National Democratic Party leader, members of Hartford's legislative delegation, some present City Council members, as well as the U. S. Congressman and Senators who represented Hartford as a part of their congressional district. Most were negative. Why not stay in the State Legislature? Why not run for City Council? I was then an assistant majority leader in the House of Representatives and had been offered an even higher position if "I behaved myself" and stayed in the legislature. I guess I misbehaved because at a meeting called by Jim Monroe with a group of community folk, we decided that I should run and that I could, and would, win. Negative responses, especially from the NAACP president, gave me a challenge that I could not refuse. My mindset went from the impossible to "why not?"

Oldest brother Marshall and Mother at Campaign Headquarters, 1981

In January of that year, over 100,000 people marched in Washington, D.C. to the nation's capitol, calling for the enactment of legislation to make the Rev. Dr. Martin Luther King's birthday a national holiday. In February of that year, our Governor Ella Grasso died from cancer, and the Rev. David Craig, founding pastor of the Mount Moriah Baptist Church, in Hartford, also died. It was also the year that the nation turned toward Atlanta, Georgia, where some twenty Black children had been slain. This became the year that I replied to those who repeatedly asked "why run for mayor? Why waste the Black vote? Why challenge the present, well-liked mayor? Why? Why? The simple answer was "Why Not?' My mayoral campaign committee adopted that slogan as our campaign theme—"Why Not Milner for Mayor?"

Wilber G. Smith, Prenzina Holloway

On a hot day in July of 1981, over one-hundred of my early supporters and family members joined me at the Old State House, in downtown
Hartford, as I formally announced my candidacy for mayor. There were
already three announced Democratic candidates: present Mayor George
Athanson, Johanna Murphy, and Richard Lawlor. Robert Ludgin, a
City Councilman, also had announced that he would be joining the
race. Polls were showing that the present mayor would easily win in a
four-way race; he was the endorsed candidate of the Democratic Party.
At that time our local daily newspaper, the *Hartford Courant*, called me
an "underdog," and I was. The campaign was on. For me it was to be
a door-to-door campaign throughout the city. Jim Monroe became my
campaign manager and we set up our headquarters in Unity Plaza, a
mini-mall on Barbour Street in the northend section of Hartford, my
base.

Early in the campaign U.S. Congressman Parren Mitchell of
Philadelphia, who I had the pleasure of meeting several times, came to
Hartford to endorse me and support my candidacy. The first union to

endorse me was the Hartford Federation of Teachers, followed by Local 1199, the Health Care Worker's Union. As I continued campaigning a group of prominent greater Hartford African American ministers publicly declared their support. Collin Bennett, the former Republican City Councilman, took me to visit the West Indian/Caribbean social clubs. It was during these visits that I received my first campaign contributions; at each club, a hat was passed around to those in attendance.

The Democratic Primary Election was held on September 8, 1981. To my surprise, and that of many others, our only daily newspaper, the *Hartford Courant*, endorsed me for mayor.

The race was on.

Election morning I was at my campaign headquarters at five o'clock. Those of us who were there first joined hands in prayer, thanking God for the opportunity. It was a hectic day. We had campaign workers at all of the polling places with their "Why Not Milner For Mayor" signs. I crisscrossed the city, stopping at just about every polling place. Most welcomed me but a few jeered. After a long day the polls finally closed at eight that night. However, by eleven o'clock, the final count had not been tallied. The media announced that it was a close race and predicted a win for Mayor Athanson.

That next morning the *Hartford Courant's* headline read "Athanson Defeats Milner by 94 Votes" and stated "Milner's strong showing was bolstered by throngs of inexperienced volunteers outperforming the Democratic Party machine on Election Day." Although we thought we had lost, it was a day of jubilation for no one thought we would even come close.

CHAPTER 13

A Court Challenge

MY ELECTION TO become mayor, however, was not over. The next morning, going over the absentee ballots (ballots that are sent in by voters who are unable to go to polls), one of my volunteers, a young lady in her teens and too young to vote, saw her grandmother's name on one of the ballots. She said her grandmother was comatose in a local convalescent home and was unable to even sign an "X" to indicate that she was capable of voting. That immediately raised a red flag.

Wilber G. Smith walked into our headquarters, heard the news, and the challenge was on. We asked for a recount but election officials ruled that a ninety-four vote margin is substantial enough for an uncontested win. Our only hope was to challenge the election through the court system, but without sound evidence we knew that it would be a waste of time.

Based on what we had heard, we decided to match our volunteers up with Justices of the Peace or Notary Publics and go from nursing home to nursing home and door to door to verify the authenticity of the absentee ballots. Calls were made and the outpour of volunteers was once again heartwarming. They paired up and fanned across the city visiting nursing homes and senior citizens whose names appeared on the absentee ballots. By the end of the day over two dozen persons were identified who were either unable to vote or who had not voted but whose names appeared having voted by absentee ballot.

The volunteers went out again the next day. By the end of that day we had identified over sixty fraudulent ballots. Because we had to go to court, we had to file before a judge. We rushed to the court house only to find that judge after judge refused to sign onto the case. We soon realized that we were not only up against our own Democratic Party but also up against judges who were appointed by Democrats and would not take a case against the Party. Just five minutes before our deadline to file we ran into Judge William Bieluch, a Superior Court judge who was about to retire. He reviewed our findings and just before the deadline, signed the necessary papers allowing us to go to court with our case. He was a Godsend.

Our next step was to obtain a lawyer. We knew that the city and the Democratic Party would call in the best lawyers they could find. Again, we ran into the same problem. Local lawyers, who were seasoned on election law, refused to take our case or challenge the Democratic Party's candidate. However a young lawyer, a Democrat by the name of Sydney Shulman agreed to file our complaint and argue the case, if necessary. Through him, we contacted a seasoned election lawyer about fifty miles away, in Bridgeport, Connecticut, by the name of Richard Beider who had a great reputation. He decided to take our case pro-bono, no charge. Our headquarters lit up with singing, crying, and jubilance. The next day's *Hartford Courant's* headline read "Milner To Sue For New Vote." Named as defendants were the Mayor, Chief Election's Moderator, our City Clerk, and the Democratic Registrar of Voters.

Another bold judge, Douglas Wright, presided over the trial. The city's attorneys tried to have the case thrown out. Instead Judge Wright, based on our evidence of improprieties, offered our campaign to either have the court rule that I was the true winner of the Democratic Primary Election or have the September election thrown out and agree to a new Democratic Primary Election on October 13th. If agreed, all four candidates would run again. We agreed and Judge Wright issued an order nullifying the original election, a first for a mayoral campaign in Connecticut history. When we left court and reached our campaign headquarters, the parking lot at Unity Plaza was packed with supporters, well wishers, and the media.

With rumors of election crimes swirling, it was reported that the City did not challenge the ruling out of fear of individuals being fined or imprisoned. This prompted the city's lawyers to agree to a new Democratic Primary Election. The next day's editorial page of our daily newspaper raised the following questions.

- Why were the voting machines not in better condition?
- Why did the mayoral candidate, the registrars of voters and the Town Clerk not make sure that the poll workers were properly trained?
- Why were voter checklist and other documents not signed properly as required by law?
- Why did officials not hasten to investigate the many apparent mistakes?
- Why did they respond only after a candidate complained?

Why, why, why? Thanks to some who believe in a just court system, we were given the opportunity to bring before the voters of Hartford the original question, "Why Not Milner For Mayor?"

The second Democratic Primary Election gained the national spotlight. Calls and support came in from across the nation to my campaign headquarters. Five of Connecticut's largest trade unions endorsed me along with Hartford's Ministerial Alliance. The Rev. A. Roger Williams of the Union Baptist Church was then president of the Alliance and one of my strongest supporters, as well as one the most respected spiritual leaders in our area. The Rev. Jesse Jackson came into town for a church rally in my support at the Horace Bushnell Church, on Albany Avenue in Harford. To forge the united effort of my campaign,

U. S. Congressman Robert Garcia of New York City held a rally to strengthen and solidify the Latino vote at the Sacred Heart Church, after an invitation from Mike Borrero, a respected community activist. Carl McCall, former Alternate Representative and New York State official, arrived in town with New York State Senator Arthur Eves and a van of volunteers from New York state. My old boss, New York City former Deputy Commissioner for Community Development, David Billings, now a Bishop in the Church of God, arrived with additional volunteers. Bus loads of volunteers arrived from Boston, Bridgeport, and New Haven. The volunteer turnout was amazing. I was most impressed by the many young volunteers; almost a half of my volunteer workers were youth not old enough to vote. They went door to door, manned the telephones, and did much of the legwork of the campaign. My other strong workforce was our volunteer senior citizens.

On that second Democratic Primary Election day in October, the voting polls opened at 6:00 A.M. At 5:00 A.M. the headquarters was jammed, with coffee and doughnuts flowing as volunteers prepared to hit the street and voting sites. It was an exciting and hectic day. I was followed by media throughout that day as I first voted then began going door to door, stopping by headquarters and trouble shooting.

When 8:00 P.M. came and the polling places closed we went to a packed campaign headquarters to await the outcome. Things were tense as poll results were posted on the large chart hanging on one of the walls. Cheers came when I was announced the winner in some, and caution and even dismay overshadowed us when I was announced the loser in others. But real jubilation came when, sometime after 9:30 P.M. and before we had all of the final results, one of the local TV stations announced that I had won the election. Cheers and tears took hold of the crowd. I was hugged and kissed and mobbed by the media as I began to thank my volunteers and to give a short victory speech.

Even though I emerged from the October Democratic Primary Election as the Democratic candidate for mayor, for the most part Hartford's Democratic Party leadership refused to accept that the majority of Democratic voters had made me their choice. We came out of the election jubilant but still optimistically cautious as we prepared for the November General Election. I faced two opponents, Bob Ludgin, who ran as an Independent, and Mike McGarry, a Republican and a member of our city council. The election drew national attention and media from throughout the country, along with a media observation team from Japan that had come into the city to watch and to report the results.

Once again I was up early election morning, a cold November day. When I arrived at headquarters around 5:20 A.M., campaign workers were already flocking in and the coffee pot was steaming. After we held hands in prayer and I finished off a cup of coffee and a doughnut, I was off to the Rawson School to cast my vote at 6 A.M. when the polling place opened. I knew that it would be a long day but an exciting one. I was taking nothing for granted but had prayed for God's will to be done.

I spent Election Day going from polling place to polling place, stopping in at headquarters to check the turnouts, make a few phone calls, and listen to my advisors. They sent me home around 7 P.M. to freshen up and to get ready to meet the press. Win or loose they would be there and win or loose I had to face them.

We had reserved the hall of the West Indian Social Club, then on Blue Hills Avenue, for the final election results. When I arrived around 8:30 P.M., the press was reporting a victory. The Hall was packed with family, friends, volunteers, and the media. Remote television vans and bright lights were everywhere in the parking lot as I was led to the Hall. All I wanted to do was to relax; I was exhausted but new energy came from the throng of cheerful well wishers and the results of the election. The next day's headlines read "Milner Makes History In New England," the same story being carried by newspapers throughout the country.

After confirmation that I had won the mayoral election, I had thanked all of my supporters and met with the throngs of media. Then a handful of close campaign workers drove me across the Connecticut river to East Hartford for a midnight snack and a chance to "chill out"

Author accepting victory, 1981 (twin nephews Carl/Clarence behind him)

away from the crowds, media, and telephones. After eating we stood on the banks of the river and looked across at the skyline of the city of Hartford. That was when it really hit me; I was elected the mayor of Connecticut's capitol city, the city of my birth, home of my mother and grandmother. But I also saw a city with many still in need, a city with the growing problems that urban centers across our nation and world were facing. It was a city of ethnic diversity and pride but also of change, and I, Thirman L. Milner, was to be its mayor.

Being the first Black mayor in New England I had no role models. I didn't even have the back-room political team that most mayors enjoy. I, a Democrat, had challenged the Democratic Party and won, but I had not won over the Democratic leadership of our city. The voters had spoken, not the so-called party bosses. I knew that the road was not going to be easy, but my life from a child on welfare to becoming mayor-elect had not been an easy road.

Prior to my election about a dozen local pastors, along with the Rev. Jesse Jackson, laid hands on me in prayer. That was power enough for me to counteract any fears that I may have had as I looked across the river at Hartford. The election had proven that the majority of the voters of Hartford were behind me, and I was confident that my faith in the same God who delivered Daniel, who opened the Red Sea, who led my ancestors from slavery, and who could make a way out of no way would be there to sustain me as long as I kept the faith and did not forget from where I came or for whom I was elected to serve.

CHAPTER 14

Inauguration Day, December 1, 1981

IT WAS A cold winter day. I found myself rushing around the city preparing for the swearing-in ceremony that evening at City Hall. I must admit I was a little nervous and apprehensive. Coming from my tailors I struck a car coming around a corner in downtown Hartford, knocking out one of its taillights and doing slight damage to my car. The arriving police officer stated he hated to start my day, and his day, by giving his future boss a ticket on the day he was being sworn in, but he did.

When I arrived at City Hall that evening it was already crowded. Family, friends, foes, the media, and well wishers were already vying for the best seats in the atrium. I was able to sneak into the City Clerk's office to freshen up and waited there for the swearing-in ceremony to begin.

By 8:00 P.M. the City Council members, Congresswoman Barbara Kennelly, Governor O'Neill, Lt. Governor Fauliso, my then pastor, the Rev. Alfred E. White, my mother, brothers, other family members, and the many other guests had taken their seats. The upstairs gallery, overlooking the atrium, was crowded with those who could not be seated and the TV lights were glaring away. It would have been a good time for me to turn around and run away, but I took my seat on the podium.

The City Clerk fist swore in the City Council members (Court of Common Council) and then I stood, nervously, to be sworn in as the 59th mayor of Hartford, and the first popularly elected African American mayor within the New England states. City Clerk, Subby Santiglia, gave me the oath of office and the proclaimed "Mr. Mayor, you are now officially in the chair." I was presented with the traditional staff that was originally carried by the first mayor of Hartford, the Honorable Thomas Seymour, and also given the symbolic key to the city of Hartford.

I then began my inaugural address as the mayor of Connecticut's capitol city. I knew that I had made my mother proud and it was my hope and prayer that I would serve in such a way as to make the people of Hartford proud. In politics you learn early that you can't please everyone, but you do your best, take the punches and keep in mind that God is the final judge of your service to mankind. I ended my address with these words.

> As we move into our most holy holiday season I ask that your prayers be with those of us who were elected to serve you as we seek to do what is best for this city and its people, a city and a people that we love. Let history show that as of this day, December 1, 1981 in seeking solutions to people problems we did not ask why, but Why Not.

Being elected New England's first popularly elected mayor of color was not an easy one for me, my family, or my campaign workers. There were hate calls, death threats, intimidation of some of the workers, innuendoes and racist comments, but in spite of it all I was elected and sworn in.

Because of the sour grapes attitudes my first day at City Hall was a surprising one. Upon arrival that morning, I found the door to the Mayor's Office locked. No one had left a key. Even the custodian had no master key that would open the door. A locksmith had to be called to remove the lock and to open the door. Inside of the office I found that every piece of paper, as well as books, files, and even official documents had been removed. The shelves and file cabinets were empty. The State Police had to go to the former mayor's residence and confiscate boxes of official city documents. Finally around 9 A.M. a lady arrived who told me that she was the mayor's secretary; I had not hired her and could not fire her. I wanted to be diplomatic on my first day in office, so I had our City Manager officially terminate her so that my own secretary could begin working for me.

My first official act was to visit the offices at City Hall and introduce myself to city staff. The welcome that I received was heartwarming, especially because I was replacing a mayor who had been at City Hall for twelve years and was quite popular. All in all, my first day was one of adjustment, meeting department heads and staff, and answering the many well wishers' calls.

The next day I rolled up my sleeves and got to work doing the job that I was elected to do on behalf of the residents of the city of Hartford. Although I was a first in New England, I had officially joined the ranks of some two hundred and fifty mayors of color in these United States.

I came into office as mayor at the same time that Hartford had its first African American city officials at other levels as well. There was W. Wilson Gaitor, our great City Manager and John B. Stewart, Hartford's first African American Fire Chief. Also, during my terms in office, three of the Deputy Mayors were of African American heritage. Frank Borges, a native Cape Verdian, was a great asset to our city and to me as Deputy Mayor, as well as a good friend. He later went on to become State Treasurer, NAACP National Treasurer, and is currently a bank president. Rudolph Arnold, an attorney, also was a good friend and great public servant. I. Charles Matthews was the third African American Deputy Mayor.

My years as mayor were also enhanced by several other city officials. Deputy Mayor Alphonse Marotta and Police Chief Bernard Sullivan both became great helpmates to me and were among those who traveled to Italy where we attended a week-long celebration with a parade during the

Swearing-in, Town Clerk Sebastian "Subby" Santiglia and Author

twinning of our two cities. Then there was our City Manager, Sebastian "Subby" Santiglia, who became my right hand in getting through the many hurdles that one faces in government.

There were many more folks at City Hall who made my job much easier, as well as many great moments during my three terms as mayor. I had the opportunity, through the National Conference of Black Mayors and the U. S. Conference of Mayors, to take several overseas fact finding and unifying trips. I traveled to the Ivory Coast of Africa, Italy, France, Germany, Taiwan, and Puerto Rico.

In Hartford a group of close friends and staff appointed themselves "The Mayor's Crew"—my cousin Barbara Wiggins, two of my Executive Assistants, Anthony Napoleon and my niece Roberta Jones, police detective Debra Callis, my close friend Ruth Hall, and Tina McDonald. They became my eyes and ears to the community and planned several events in my behalf. They were a fun group who remained close long after I left office, even to this day.

I also became First Vice President of the National Conference of Black Mayors (NCMB). Marion Barry, then mayor of Washington, D.C., served as president of the organization. During my second term

Author at City Hall presenting proclamation (l-r) Samuel Thomas, Irvin Beck, Mayor Milner, Richard Reddin, Anthony J. Napoleon

in office I brought the Annual Conference of the NCBM to Hartford. It was the first time that many of the members had been north and the first time that Hartford residents had seen that many African American mayors. It was a great week-long event.

At the end of my terms in office one of my Executive Assistants, Anthony Napoleon, went on to join the Hartford Fire Department and the Mayor's Crew planned a successful retirement banquet for me. At that point I also held the position of Director of Government Affairs for Edward's Supermarket, and served as Chairman of the Government Relation's Committee of the Food Market Institute, in Washington, D.C. The Committee was composed mainly of CEO's, V.P.'s, and Directors from most of this nation's major supermarkets. I was the only African American serving, and it was a rewarding experience.

Although this book is not about my personal life, during my first term as mayor I married for the second time. Brenda Monterio was the widow of a former City Councilman and a mother of three, whom I had met at the State Capitol during my term as State Representative. We had a great wedding, honeymooned in Jamaica, and settled down in a home on Colebrook Street, in Hartford, along with my mother and my wife's teenage daughter.

CHAPTER 15

The Thirman L. Milner Core Knowledge Academy

IN 1988 THREE African American members of the Hartford Board of Education, Thelma Dickerson, Courtney Gardner, and Sandra Little expressed their desire to name one of Hartford's public schools in my honor. At first I was reluctant, mainly due to the fact that a public school had never been named after a living person in Hartford.

I thought about all of the ramifications that would go with such a naming. First of all it would put me in the spotlight for the remainder of my life; I would automatically become a role model, at least to the students of that school. I also knew that I would become personally involved with the school and the students. This would be a heavy undertaking on my part. However, the three members of the board felt that, because of my commitment to youth and education, they wanted to bestow this honor upon me.

After giving it much thought and sharing the proposal with family members I accepted the offer, or I guess I should say, honor. The resolution was put before the entire board and passed without exception. There was a one-year waiting period for public response and input. The year went by without any objection and the resolution to rename the Vine Street School in Hartford, the *Thirman L. Milner Elementary School* was passed.

The Vine Street School was located in one of the most depressed and poorest areas of Hartford. At the time the school went from kindergarten to the sixth grade, with about five-hundred students, of which 99 percent were of African American and Hispanic heritage. Many of these students had only their moms at home. I had grown up in a similar community. Coming from a single parent home with my family on welfare (as many of these student's families were) I felt that, considering my family background, if renaming the school could bring hope and change to these students and the school community, then it would be a worthwhile honor. Under Principal William Chambers, there was a great renaming ceremony in which the students participated and performed roles portraying me from my early days to the day I became mayor. The event was attended by my family members, parents, students, and community folk, including U. S. Congresswoman Barbara Kennelly who represented the District and was also a friend and former City Councilwoman.

Along with other organizations, each year during the sixth-grade promotional exercises the Milner family presented the "Thirman L. Milner Student Achiever Award," a certificate and monetary contribution to two students who showed the most improvement during their stay at Milner. There was also the establishment of the Milner School Community Board that I co-chaired along with Hattie Harris, a long-time community activist, who was then president of the Vine Street Task Force (the school was located on Vine Street). We met monthly to determine how we could best assist the school, the students, and the school community. The board consisted of community activists, representatives of social organizations, and school staff. We conducted cookouts for the students on the school grounds at the end of the school year. We held movie nights at the school and sought outside support for activities, grants, and services, such as tutoring and mentoring.

In the year 2008 the school was renamed the *Thirman L. Milner Core Knowledge Academy*, adopting an education concept that had been successful in many other cities. The Core Knowledge concept was a new learning experience for the school staff as well as the students, and challenged everyone to increase the academic quality of the school.

The *Thirman L. Milner Core Knowledge Academy* has now added pre-kindergarten and seventh and eight grades. There are some four-hundred students, some who come with home and community based problems, but all are great kids who just need an equal opportunity to learn and to succeed. My hope and prayer is that the *Thirman L. Milner Core Knowledge Academy* will give them that hope and the opportunity to succeed.

CHAPTER 16

The State Senate Election and a New Era

A FEW YEARS after I had left the mayor's office, my good friend, Wilber G. Smith, told me that he was going to run for his old State Senate seat in the 1992 election. Since leaving the State Senate Wilber had remained a community activist and served as president of our local NAACP Branch. He was highly outspoken and held in high esteem, and of course had my full support. Sadly, a year before the election he announced that he had cancer; but with his strong will and determination he continued his campaign.

It was just a few months before the September Democratic Primary Election that he was first confined to his bed at home; he remained upbeat about his recovery and ongoing campaign. In early August of that year, I paid one of my regular visits to his bedside. He was not as upbeat as usual. His sister said that he would not eat. She gave me his plate and he did take a few bites of his food, gave me one of his usual sly smiles, and pushed the plate away. He said, "Sit down, we need to talk." I sat and he looked at me and said, "I need you to do me a favor."

"No problem," I said. "What is it?"

"I want you to run in my place, I won't be able to do it."

Although I knew the gravity of his illness I was not ready for his words. I told him he would be okay; he just needed to eat and get his strength back. He smiled again and said, "just promise me you will run in my place." I told him to get some rest, eat, and we both had time to think about the election.

A week, or so, later he went to the hospital and then moved to the Veteran's Hospital in Newington, Connecticut. It was there, knowing of his fading condition, that I promised him I would run for the Senate in his place. This was end of June of that year and the Democratic Primary Election was in September. I pulled together "the Mayor's Crew." With the help and encouragement of young talent like Shawn Wooden, who went on to become an attorney, Dorothy Payne, who had opened her home to me during my first election campaign for State Representative, my cousin Barbara Wiggins, and a few more of my old friends and supporters, we organized our campaign.

Brother Gary, Atty. Cynthia Jennings, Author, Atty. Shawn Wooden,
Campaign Headquarters for State Senate

In August, the day before the West Indian Day Celebration Parade, Wilber died. I was called to his home early that night where his family and friends had gathered. Although expected, it was a tough night for all of us but I had to keep my promise to him. The next morning the Crew and some of my campaign volunteers gathered at my campaign headquarters where we decided to still participate in the parade. We quickly put together a few campaign posters with Wilber's picture on them to wear on the front of our chests as we marched, along with black ribbons tied around our arms. For me, and I am sure for many of those who marched with our group, it was the saddest parade of my life. We walked the entire route and Wilber was given recognition as we passed the reviewing stand. For many in the parade crowd our signs were their first knowledge that Wilber had passed, although it had been on the early TV news and in our daily newspaper.

In September of that year I won the Democratic Primary Election and went on to win the General Election in November. I kept my promise to Wilber by serving one term as State Senator before going into semi-retirement in 1994.

Although going through several stages of several illnesses over the many years since 1994, I remained active in my community and church. I served for a two-year period as president of our local branch of the NAACP, then attended the Hartford Seminary, after which I became an exhorter and then a local preacher. I served the church of my birth, Metropolitan AME Zion, and served for a short term as Interim Executive Director of one of our small, local community service agencies, ONE/CHANE. I then became involved in state and local coordinating positions with the campaigns of the Rev. Jesse Jackson for President,

Ned Lamont for Governor of Connecticut, and as a supporter of the campaign of Barack Obama for president.

In the spring of 2008 I had the pleasure of meeting Barack Obama at one of his fundraisers at the home of Frank Borges, a bank president, who once served as Deputy Mayor during one of my terms as mayor. Thanks to the kindness of Connecticut Congressman John Larson, whom I had known for many years, I had the opportunity to attend the Democratic National Convention in Denver, Colorado, that year. Former mayor Carrie Saxon Perry also joined me. She became New England's first popularly elected female African American mayor after I endorsed her when I decided to step down in 1987.

Attending that convention, where Obama gave his great speech as the Democratic candidate for President, and the election of President Barack Obama, were what I would call the climax of my involvement in the civil rights struggle. I never thought that, during my lifetime, we could and would elect a president of African heritage. It is a proud moment in the history of our country, the world, and for me. Even though I consider his election the apex of my personal civil rights involvement, as long as I have breath I will continue my civil rights and community service as well as political advising. For me, President Obama's election highlighted the fruit of the years of struggle of my ancestors, from the slaveship to freedom. It was the crowning point of my involvement in the civil rights movement to my election as the first popularly elected mayor of African American heritage within the New England states of these United States. It was also a great victory for the untold thousands who sacrificed their lives. They enabled me to say "Why Not?", for President Obama to say "Yes We Can!", and for America to say "Yes We Did!"

About the Author

The Honorable Thirman L. Milner was born in Hartford, Connecticut, on October 29, 1933, to Henry Marshall Milner and Grace Nelson Milner, the next youngest of nine children. A third generation native of Hartford and eighth generation in Connecticut on his mother's side, his ancestry dates back to days of slavery in Middlesex County—now Middletown, Connecticut—and to the Native American Wongunk Tribe.

In 1981 Milner became the first popularly elected mayor of African American heritage within the New England states, serving three terms. His community service began when he became a civil rights and community activist, during the 1950's and '60's, demonstrating and marching with the late Dr. Martin Luther King, Jr., Rev. Jesse Jackson, the Honorable Andrew Young, Wilber G. Smith, and many others. Prior to being elected mayor, he served as a State Representative. Several years after leaving the mayor's office he was elected a State Senator, and appointed to serve as an assistant majority leader in both the House and Senate.

Milner served in the following positions during his career: First Vice President of the National Conference of Black Mayors; Director of Government Affairs for Edward's Super Food Stores; Chairman of the Government Relations Committee of the Food Marketing Institute, Washington, D. C.; Vice Chairman of the Board of Directors of the Connecticut Food Association and on the Boards of the New York and the Massachusetts State Food Associations; Deputy Assistant Commissioner for Community Development, New York City; District 1199, Drug Division, Union Delegate, New York City; Executive Assistant to Chairman David Billings, New York City Council Against Poverty; Interim Executive Director, Cabaleros Hispanos, Brooklyn, New York; Communications Director for the Community Renewal Team of Greater Hartford; Interim Executive Director of the Hartford community Organization, ONE CHANE; a Corporator of Saint Francis Hospital and the Hartford Public Library.

Milner is a tribal member of the Nehantic-Wongunk Confederacy; a Prince Hall Mason, Excelsior Lodge; member of the Sons of the American Revolution; a graduate of the F. B. I. Citizen's Academy; Life Member of the National Association for the Advancement of Colored People (NAACP) and past President of the Greater Hartford Branch; graduate of the Hartford Seminary's Black Ministries Certificate Program; and life-long member of the Metropolitan A. M. E. Zion Church, having served as a local preacher.

Milner received numerous awards, citations, and tributes throughout his years of public, community, and civil rights service, among them the renaming of the Vine Street School, in 1989, the Thirman L. Milner Elementary School. His numerous awards include the Marcus Garvey Community Service Award; the establishment of a Thirman L. Milner Scholarship, donated by Heublien Corporation through the University of Hartford; the NAACP's Roy Wilkins' Distinguished Service Award; and the Jewish Tree of Life Award.

LaVergne, TN USA
19 January 2010
170539LV00001B/7/P